COWBOYS
AND
KANSAS

COWBOYS
AND
KANSAS

*Stories from the
Tallgrass Prairie*

BY JIM HOY

UNIVERSITY OF OKLAHOMA PRESS
NORMAN AND LONDON

By Jim Hoy
(with John Somer) *The Language Experience* (New York, 1974)
The Cattle Guard: Its History and Lore (Lawrence, 1982)
Cassoday, Cow Capital of Kansas (El Dorado, Kansas, 1984)
(with Tom Isern) *Plains Folk: A Commonplace of the Great Plains*
(Norman, 1987)
(with Tom Isern) *Plains Folk II: The Romance of the Landscape*
(Norman, 1990)
Riding Point: A Centennial History of the Kansas Livestock Association
(Fargo, 1994)
Cowboys and Kansas: Stories from the Tallgrass Prairie (Norman, 1995)

Library of Congress Cataloging-in-Publication Data

Hoy, James F.
 Cowboys and Kansas : stories from the Tallgrass Prairie / by Jim
Hoy.
  p.   cm.
 Includes index.
 ISBN: 0–8061–2688–4 (alk. paper, hardcover)
 ISBN: 0–8061–2867–4 (alk. paper, paperback)
  1. Cowboys—Kansas—History. 2. Cowgirls—Kansas—History.
 3. Ranch life—Kansas—History. 4. Kansas—History. I. Title.
 F681.H69 1995
 978.1—dc20
                                                         94–29789
                                                              CIP

The paper in this book meets the guidelines for permanence and
durability of the Committee on Production Guidelines for Book
Longevity of the Council on Library Resources, Inc.♾

2   3   4   5   6   7   8   9   10

For Kenneth, Marshall, and Josh

Contents

"KANSAS," wrote historian Carl Becker, "is a state of mind."
So is a cowboy. The real combines with the mythic, the historical with the contemporary, to create an image in the mind's
eye. We know what a cowboy looks like. We know how one
acts, how he dresses, what he does, where he can be found.
But as with many images created primarily in the imagination (whether individual or collective), the truth is often
more complex.

Let me cite an example, a man who was one of our neighbors when I was growing up. Toad Griffin was a cowboy. But
you never would have known it by looking at him. Toad was
not exactly fat, but he had a belly on him, and he was round
faced, not slim and hard and lean. Toad wore bib overalls
much of the time, or off-brand jeans, not trim-fitting Levi's.
His boots were usually Acmes, if he wasn't wearing work
shoes. His horse (he usually had only one at any particular
time—Whitey and Buck, in that order, were the last two he
owned) was invariably fat and lazy. Toad wouldn't, couldn't,
spring lightly into the saddle, like a cowboy. He'd hunt for a
ditch to stand Whitey in, then haul himself on by the saddle
strings, pulling the saddle halfway down the horse's side at
the same time. He couldn't have stayed with a bucking horse
for more than a jump or two if his life depended on it. In
fact, he rarely got his horse out of a trot. His old grass rope
was always raggy, but then he never roped anything anyway,
might even have had trouble swinging the loop over his head.
Which was fine with me, because I always got the call to come
over and rope the foot-rot steers in the Hupp Pastures that he
looked after. When we worked calves, Toad would sit on a
feed bunk and load the vaccinating syringes while others did
the more strenuous, and exciting, jobs. No, he didn't look
like much of a cowboy, or act like one, either. But my adolescent scorn for surface appearances, including Toad's, soon
gave way to understanding and even admiration. He had,

after all, spent his entire life looking after cattle on the tall-grass prairie, and he could tell wonderful tales of the early days of meeting the Texas steers at the Newton stockyards, then trailing them for two or three days to put them into their summer pastures east of Cassoday.

I remember once my Uncle Marshall, who both looked like a cowboy ought to look and was a genuine hand, pasture and arena, telling of a time when he and Toad and some younger cowboys were working calves south of Aikman, a watering stop and stockyards on the Santa Fe south of town. Toad, as was his wont, was loading syringes and moving slow while some of the young toughs ran calves into the chute and others helped Uncle Marshall with the branding and dehorning. Some of them began to make fun of Toad, which didn't bother him any. He defined the term "equanimity"; I don't remember ever seeing him mad or upset. (And darn sure not excited. Toad worked for the maintenance crew on the Kansas Turnpike, and I did, too, one summer. We would be in a dump truck ten or twelve miles out at about 3:30 in the afternoon, and he'd start driving back to headquarters. He never stopped, and we'd pull into the garage about a quarter till five, just in time to get ready to leave for the day. I remember when he had a mild heart attack and the doctor told him he'd have to slow down. The whole town wondered how in hell he could go any slower!) The mockery was not overtly malicious, but Uncle Marshall, who could get stirred up, could take only so much of it before rising in Toad's defense: "You young bucks think you're pretty hot stuff, but I'll tell you all one thing. If I had to move this bunch of cows from here to Cassoday I could do it a whole lot easier with just Toad helping than with all the rest of you put together, running your horses around and whooping up the cattle. He might not get his horse out of a trot, but by golly he wouldn't have to. He knows what a cow is going to do before she does it, and he'll be in the right place at the right time. Why, he's more of a cowboy than any of you guys ever will be!"

No, being a cowboy is not just appearance, despite the way

all the country singers, truck drivers, and urban cowboys get dolled up. Part of it is in knowing how to do the job; there's no higher praise among working cowboys than being accepted as a hand. The scorn of things noncowboy shown by the young twisters that Uncle Marshall rebuked is typical of cowboys—theirs was just misapplied. Being able to saddle and ride a horse, round up and drive cattle, help with branding and loading, fix a water gap or a windmill—all these skills help to mark a true cowboy. But that's not all of it.

There's the attitude. When I worked on the Rogler Ranch, one of the hands was more interested in farming than ranching. He was good enough in helping with cattle, but his real interest was in the cornfields along the Southfork River, not the bluestem that rose in the pastures above the stream. And I have known farm boys who had cowboy in their hearts and who were top ropers and riders, even if they couldn't earn their living following a chuck wagon on one of the big Texas or Montana spreads.

There just isn't room for too many cowboys, real working cowboys, in the world, you see. There are only so many ranches and so many cattle to be tended from horseback. And only so many men, and women, who are willing to take the physical stress or to make the financial sacrifice of living on cowboy wages. Like Old Lodge Skins says about the Cheyenne in Thomas Berger's *Little Big Man,* "There have always been a limited number of Human Beings." There are sure-enough working cowboys still to be found throughout the West, if you follow Baxter Black's advice and get off the highways and onto the back roads to look for them. But there are other cowboys as well, those who have earned their spurs but no longer wear them on a quotidian basis, those who have cowboy in their hearts but have chosen (or have had chosen for them) another way to make a living. "Are you a cowboy?" the third-graders ask me after I have spent an hour showing them slides of old-time cowboys, singing them cowboy folk-songs, and showing-and-telling them spurs, branding iron, and rope. Yes, I suppose so, even though my salary comes not from riding, but from writing and teaching. I take my blood from those who did excel at this, and I have earned my living from the back of a horse.

I have also spent some little time delving into the history of the cowboy, both through books and through talking with old-timers. The essays and stories in this collection are thus the result of both personal experience and inquiry. My perspective is that of a tallgrass native and a Kansas patriot; my home state, I believe, deserves more recognition for the role it has played in the development of the cowboy, an omission I occasionally attempt to rectify in print. Some of the material in this collection has appeared in the newspaper column "Plains Folk," which Tom Isern and I write; some has been gleaned from my column "Cattle Country" in the late (and sorely missed) *KS. Magazine*; some has been published in *The Cattleman, Kanhistique, Kansas Heritage, The Longhorn Scene,* and *Persimmon Hill*; and some has not before been published. Where it might help to avoid confusion, I have noted, at the beginning of the selection, the date of initial composition.

A collection of this sort is something like a catch-all pasture stocked with different breeds, weights, and kinds of cattle. Some essays are short, some are longer; some are humorous, some are more serious; some are casual, some are more formal. Just as you can shape up a diverse herd of cattle in different ways—by throwing similar sizes together, or similar colors, or types, or sexes, or brands—so in this book I have chosen to arrange the contents by brand and by type: sections that correspond roughly to people, animals, work, play, and equipment.

JIM HOY
from the Flint Hills

Part One

KANSAS COWBOYS

KANSAS. What image comes to mind? Wheat fields and sunflowers. Farmers with straws sticking out of their mouths. Carry Nation and sod houses and John Brown and grasshoppers and tornadoes. Cornfields and General Eisenhower and windmills and grain elevators and William Allen White. All good images, and true.

But be honest. How many think of cowboys when they think of Kansas? Well, they should. Without Kansas, the cowboy as we know him—America's greatest folk hero, the core of our national identity, the embodiment of our philosophy of self reliance—would never have come into existence. Now there are all kinds of cowboys—working cowboys (both contemporary and old-time), rodeo cowboys, movie cowboys, television cowboys, pulp-western cowboys, singing cowboys, drugstore cowboys, urban cowboys, line-dance cowboys, weekend cowboys—but the most important, in my opinion, are the working cowboy (i.e., the *real* cowboy) and the cowboy of popular culture (i.e., the *mythic* cowboy). Both are genuine, of course, only in different ways. The working cowboy is the real-life cowboy, the one who earns his living on a ranch or, in the old days, earned it as a drover. He receives, and has always received, relatively small wages, but something about the nature of the job attracts him and stays with him, even if he quits and takes up town work. The mythic cowboy, on the other hand, is just as real, even though many of his attributes (the fast draw, the face-off on Main Street at high noon, the commitment to Justice) are the work of fiction. The mythic cowboy is real because he embodies our national character, both good and bad. The term "cowboy" can be pejorative or it can be laudatory. Teddy Roosevelt, "that cowboy in the White House," could act impulsively and with little regard for legal niceties ("speak softly and carry a big stick," especially if, for instance, you are going to establish Panama as an independent country because it will be easier to deal with than Colombia), but he could also act humanely and justly (as, for instance, when he was busting trusts or establishing national parks).

The image of the cowboy, in fact, is so pervasive that it has become the unofficial symbol of our country. Want to be recognized anywhere in the world as an American? Wear a cowboy hat. Want to welcome a visiting dignitary by making him an honorary American? Put a cowboy hat on his head and shoot some footage for the six o'clock news. The image of the cowboy is so powerful, so engrained in our cultural being and imagination, that when Henry Kissinger was interviewed by Oriana Fallaci a couple of decades ago, when he was asked by the incisive Italian journalist how he perceived himself, he replied that he was like the cowboy who rode into town, faced down the bad guys, then rode off into the sunset. Or words to that effect. Now think of that for a moment. Let the full import and impact sink in. Here is Henry Kissinger, at the time Richard Nixon's secretary of state, arguably the third or fourth most politically powerful man on earth, the opener of China, the winner of the Nobel Peace Prize, Henry Kissinger with his heavy German accent, a European Jew, Harvard intellectual, Washington insider, and jetsetter who dated movie stars. When asked to describe his modus operandi, he responds by likening himself to a cowboy, to a hired-man-on-horseback, to a dollar-a-day drover. Of course he had in mind the mythic cowboy, but even that incarnation of our national psyche is firmly founded in the young boys who followed the herds north from Texas to Kansas.

Oh yes, Kansas. Remember? Without Kansas the cowboy *as we know him* would never have come into existence. The cattle were in Texas, but the cow towns were in Kansas. There have been plenty of mounted herders throughout history and throughout the world, but it was the post–Civil War trail drive that created the cowboy as we recognize him today. The steppes of central Asia had been home to nomadic herders for centuries; cattle stations had been established in Australia before our Civil War; Spanish America, in both continents, had long had a cattle industry (and contributed both equipment design and work methods to the North American cowboy); even Hawaii had had cowboys (*paniolos*, they were called) thirty years before we did. As David Dary in *Cowboy Culture* and Terry Jordan in *Trails to Texas* point out, various forces and influences—Spanish, English, European—came together in Texas to foster our cattle industry. But it was the big trail drives after the Civil War that provided the crucible wherein the cowboy was formed, where the myth was forged. And it was the journalists, gone west after the war in search of new adventures to stir their readers, and their own adrenalin, who transformed the dusty drover, blowing off steam in the squalid cow town dance halls, into the rough-and-ready, raring-and-tearing cowboy. The exciting image they drew captured the public imagination almost immediately, and the fascination has endured.

Cattle had been driven from Texas before the Civil War, sometimes driven long distances. To the California gold fields in the early 1850s, for instance, or to markets in the East. But usually in small numbers and sometimes even on foot. After the Civil War, however, huge herds were put together and driven north to the railheads of Kansas. The reason was simple: economics. Cattle had multiplied rapidly during the war and few had been sold or otherwise removed from the range. At war's end steers worth only a few dollars in Texas could bring ten or twenty times that in Chicago or St. Louis. It didn't take long for entrepreneurs to put together sizable droves—one thousand, two thousand, three thousand head or more—and move them toward those markets.

The first big drives were in 1866 along the Shawnee Trail, out of Texas, through Indian Territory and southeastern Kansas, and into Missouri. Older readers, and younger ones with cable television, will recall that Rowdy Yates and Gil Favor of "Rawhide" (Clint Eastwood's big break into show business) were driving their cattle to Sedalia, Missouri. In the movies and on television the cowboy is rough and tough, quick with his fists and fast with his gun, always ready to take on the bad guys to champion justice or fair maiden. That is one of the key features of the mythic cowboy, and the plot of a thousand Westerns. Just think of *Shane,* with Alan Ladd riding in to help the homesteaders triumph over the evil Jack Palance, then riding off into the sunset, a wound in his side but nobility in his heart. If the placid, easy-going farmer gets into trouble, then the cowboy has to come along and get him out.

But in real life it didn't work out that way. The Missouri farmer was more than a match for the Texas drover. The Missourians didn't like the Texas longhorns tromping their crops, tearing up their fields, eating their grass, infecting their domestic cattle with Texas fever. So they chased the cowboys, caught them, tied them up to trees and rail fences, horsewhipped them, and threatened to shoot them if they ever came back. They didn't.

In the meantime, a man from Illinois named Joseph G. McCoy had come out into Kansas, approaching officials of the Kansas Pacific Railroad and convincing them that if they would build loading pens the cattle would come and the railroad would make lots of money. Somehow, although he owned no cattle, he successfully parlayed his field of dreams into a reality and headed west to build pens. He stopped at Salina, but folks there didn't want them. So he went back east to Junction City, but folks there had Fort Riley. What did they need of cattle pens? Then he went to a little village about halfway between those two cities, a town so small (only twelve houses) that they couldn't stop him. Abilene, the first cow town. McCoy built the pens, then sent a scout, William Suggs, down toward Texas, hunting cattle. There he found, in Indian Territory, a big drove being grazed. The trail boss was afraid to go into Missouri, taking his chances with the Indians rather than the Missouri farmers. Bring 'em to Abilene, Suggs said.

He did, and the floodgates opened. For five years Abilene was the major cattle-shipping point in the nation. Hundreds of thousands of head passed through the town on their way to the Kansas City market and points east. Abilene became the prototype of the cow town—saddlers, bootmakers, and other outfitters set up shop; gambling halls, saloons, and whorehouses did a land-office business; drunken cowhands blew their pay while stern lawmen (men like "Bear River" Tom Smith, the marshal without a gun, or Wild Bill Hickok, the consummate gunfighter) strove to control the violence.

And then Abilene grew and, in a pattern to be repeated throughout the West, the citizens rebelled against the violence and the disorder. The railroads extended their lines, and the cow towns moved. Now, every state in the West had cow towns—Fort Worth, Texas, and Old Tascosa out in the Panhandle; Magdalena, New Mexico; Cheyenne, Wyoming; Miles City, Montana; Ogallala, Nebraska—but Kansas had more than any other state. Abilene, Baxter Springs, Coffeyville, Wichita, Hunnewell, Caldwell, Newton, Ellis, Hays City, Waterville, Brookville, Great Bend, Spearville, Raymond, Elgin, Ellsworth—and the Queen of them all, Dodge City.

Dodge City. Rowdiest town in Kansas. Toughest town in the West. Meanest place in the country. Wildest town in the world. I remember reading in *The Trail Drivers of Texas* about a drunk cowboy who got on a train in Wichita. The conductor came along collecting tickets, but the drunken cowhand didn't have one. "So where are you going?" asked the conductor. "I'll sell you one." "I'm a goin' to hell," was the cowboy's response. "Dodge City, two dollars," replied the conductor, and sent him on down the road.

Dodge had the reputation, all right, and it still does, thanks to "Gunsmoke." Back in the early 1970s one of my colleagues in the English Department at Emporia State University went to France on sabbatical. A linguist, he was studying language in a little town so provincial that people there had heard of only two cities in America: New York and Dodge City. "Gunsmoke" was a staple on their local television.

If you watch an hour of "Gunsmoke," it will usually start with somebody getting killed, then the bad guys will murder two or three more during the course of the show, and at the end Matt Dillon will have to face down the villains in a big shoot-out on the streets of Dodge. So at the end of an hour (actually about forty seven minutes taking out the commercials), there are six or eight bodies to be carted up to Old Boothill. I don't want to be misunderstood: there was violence and brutality in the world of the cowboy. Stampedes killed cowhands, and so did rattlesnakes and Indians and outlaws and other cowhands. Cowboys loved their guns. But they generally carried them in the chuck wagon while on the trail, then collected them, and their pay, once they reached town and went in for a bath, a spree, and a little target shooting, usually at street lights. When they did shoot at one another, they often missed because the pistols were notoriously inaccurate, even if the cowboys had been sober and good shots, which most of them weren't, on either account. Not only that, but after a couple of blasts of that old black powder, they wouldn't have been able to see what they were shooting at anyway. Let me repeat; there *was* violence and gunplay in the cow towns. Just not nearly as much as you'd expect from watching television or going to the movies. In fact, a historian friend of mine who has looked into these matters says that he can document an average of one and a half violent deaths per year in the cow towns during the time that they were cow towns. That's a heck of a lot less than the six or eight in less than an hour of "Gunsmoke." He also says that he can prove without doubt (there may have been more, but not clearly documented) that Wild Bill Hickok, the most famous gunfighter of the Old West, killed only two men in his tenure as marshal of Abilene. And one of those was his own deputy, whom he shot by accident. That the city fathers of Wichita got so upset by one murder that they hired Wyatt Earp to come in and clean up the town, or that Newton, as a result of the eight deaths that occurred there in the one year it was a cow town, acquired the nickname "Bloody Newton," says something about how our popular culture has exaggerated the bloodshed.

The old-time cowboy did sometimes meet a violent death, but usually from an accident, not from a gunshot. In fact, from my reading of *The Trail Drivers of Texas,* I would say that the most common cause of death among drovers was drowning, along with getting struck by lightning. To get the cattle north to Kansas, the cowboys had to bring them across what Harry Chrisman called the "ladder of rivers," and because most of the herds were moved up in the spring or early summer, when rainfall is the heaviest on the plains, they had to swim the Red and the Cimarron and the Arkansas and the Salt Fork.

Bringing the cattle up in the spring. That reminds me of another reason that Kansas, along with Texas, deserves credit for the birth of the cowboy. The cattle, large numbers as noted, were in Texas, and the cow towns were in Kansas. But it wasn't just the cow towns that drew them here. In fact, cattle could have been shipped by rail from Texas during the period of the great cattle drives. But the railheads were in east Texas and the freight rates were so high that it was easier and cheaper for cattle owners to hire a crew of eight or ten men plus a cook and a horse wrangler to drive the cattle to Kansas than it was to ship them from Texas. But there was another, more important, economic reason for bringing them north.

Grass.

Texas can produce lots of cattle, and grow them up to three or four year olds, but it's hard to fatten a steer on sand, sagebrush, and mesquite. The herds, driven in the early years mostly by single young men, most of them from Texas and the South, but others from all over (Missouri, Iowa, Kansas, Nebraska, Indiana), would be started north in early spring, arriving in Kansas in May or June. But they often wouldn't be sold until September or October, or even until the following spring. In other words, it was the Kansas cow towns and the Kansas grass—the tallgrass of the Flint Hills, the tall and mixed grass of the Smoky and Gypsum hills, the buffalo grass of the High Plains—that drew the herds from Texas.

Later, of course, the cattle would be taken on north—to Nebraska, the Dakotas, Wyoming, Montana, and Canada—and with them the cowboy and his folk culture would spread into those parts of the more colorful West. But this culture had its start in Kansas and Texas. Even the high-heeled Texas cowboy boot began in Kansas (see chapter 41). Today the cowboy, from vaquero to buckaroo, can be found throughout the West. In the popular mind cowboy country might be equated with Arizona or Utah or Texas or Montana, but Kansas and the tallgrass deserves recognition, too. Good cowboys can be found wherever there are cattle to be worked, the nature of that work varying somewhat from region to region, but don't let anyone tell you that Kansas isn't cowboy country. This, after all, is where it all began.

2. *Kansas Rodeo Champions*

(November 1985)

OUTSIDERS don't often think of Kansas as a cowboy state, nor, apparently, do we ourselves. Wheat State, the Sunflower State, the Land of Ahs. In a way this is an advantage; we have not suffered from the phony cowboyization that afflicts many of the states to the west of us. Haven't you ever noticed that every lawyer from Wyoming, every doctor in Montana—in fact, every civil servant west of the Pecos—affects boots and hat, even if he has never been on a horse in his life? At least it seems that way to me.

But Kansas, where we tend to underplay rather than brag about our strengths, has as much right to claim cowboy culture as an essential part of its character as any other state— and more than most. We might not have as many acres of rangeland as most western states, but our three major grazing areas—the Flint Hills, the Smoky Hills, and the Red Hills (or Gypsum Hills, as they are often called)—have such good and abundant grass that Kansas consistently ranks as one of the top cattle-producing states in the nation.

Besides, if it had not been for Kansas—and Texas—there would not have been a Great American Cowboy. Admittedly this powerful mythic figure bears little physical (or moral) resemblance to the hired man on horseback who, after the Civil War, trailed cattle from the vast ranges of Texas to the railheads in Kansas, fattening them on our rich grasses along the way, but these were his origins. With the help of eastern journalists, dime novelists, and entrepreneurs of Wild West shows, the dust-eating, bone-wearied drovers of the open

range had become the gun-toting, justice-bringing cowboy
heroes of our dreams by the time the frontier closed.

By this time, too, the railroads and the Homestead Act
had filled Kansas with wheat-growing immigrants, people
who thought cows were for milking, pigs were for eating, and
cowboys were for keeping in Texas or sending on to Montana. As a result, much of the cowboy mystique—at least in
the popular mind—has passed us by. Television stand-up co-
medians (those great barometers of national stereotypes)
think of us as a state of farmers in bib overalls with straws
stuck in our teeth.

But in real life, it just isn't so. The Flint Hills, the Gyp
Hills, the Smoky Hills, and the High Plains are filled with
working cowboys, and while we haven't produced a movie
cowboy to compare with Gene Autry or a singing cowboy to
compare with Marty Robbins, we have had our share of top
rodeo cowboys.

In fact, when it comes to producing world-champion cowboys, Kansas is right up there. The first official records of
world champions start with 1929. Before that time various
top rodeos declared their own world champions. I don't
know if any Kansans ever won any of these championships,
but I do know that Fred Beeson of Arkansas City was one of
the top steer ropers of the early years of this century and that
Cliff King and Dan Offutt, both of Garden City, were top
bronc riders who competed throughout the country. And
there were lots of others.

What I didn't know (and I'll bet most other people didn't
know either), is that Kansas has been home to more world-
champion cowboys than all but four other states. Based on
my survey of records provided by the Professional Rodeo
Cowboys Association (PRCA), and counting only individuals
who have won titles and not total number of titles won, only
Oklahoma (with thirty-three champions), Texas (with twenty-
nine), California (with twenty-four), and New Mexico (with
thirteen) outrank Kansas, with its eight title winners.

That's right—some of the great popular-culture bastions
of cowboyhood bring up the rear: Utah hasn't had any world-

champion rodeo cowboys; Nebraska and British Columbia
have had but one each; Nevada and North Dakota have had
two each; Washington has had three; South Dakota and Wyoming five each; Alberta, Oregon, and Montana six each; and
Idaho seven. Arizona ties with Kansas.

Now anybody who makes up lists has had to do some
playing around with statistics, so I'd better explain my figures. I counted winners in the five standard events (bareback, saddle bronc, and bull riding; calf roping and steer
wrestling) and the classic from the early days—single-steer
roping. I also counted in a couple of Kansans who had
moved on to other states by the time they won their titles.

Complicating the process was the mess the PRCA made of
things during 1976, 1977, and 1978 when they declared both
PRCA champions (based on yearly winnings—the traditional
determinant) and world champions (based on winnings at
the National Finals Rodeo). Fortunately, they returned to
their senses, and the standard method of naming champions,
in 1979.

Nineteen seventy-nine. That was the year that Bobby Berger, my old coyote- and coon-hunting pardner from Halstead
(although by then transplanted to Oklahoma), won the saddle-
bronc championship in probably the closest race in PRCA
history; only five dollars separated him from second-place finisher Tom Miller of South Dakota. But if ever anyone deserved
a championship, it was Bob. Two years earlier he had ended
the regular season leading the standings (by unusual coinci-
dence, again by only five dollars), but had not had good finals
and so had to settle for the PRCA championship.

I first met Bobby when his family started coming to Wilber
Countryman's Fourth of July rodeo at Cassoday, one of the
last big open-to-the-world ranch rodeos of its time. Bob's
older brothers, Kenny and Donny, were also top riders. In
fact, Don was one of the best four-event cowboys (he did
everything but rope calves) you'll ever find. So Bobby's world
championship was one I really savored.

Five years earlier another friend had won the saddle-bronc
title, setting a new earnings record in the process. John

McBeth is originally from Kingman, where his grandfather in 1899 helped found the Kingman Cattleman's Picnic, the first modern rodeo in Kansas. John's dad, Harold, was a professional calf roper from the 1930s to the 1950s, so John comes by his rodeoing naturally. I was about a year ahead of John in school, and when I first met him he was riding barebacks and roping calves in high school rodeos. When he started riding saddle broncs, however, he found his true calling and became a one-event specialist. John lives in Burden now, where he has a western store, makes saddles, and braids bull ropes and buck reins.

A lot of rodeo cowboys I have known have been superstitious, but John McBeth is the only one I have ever seen who could leap all the way across a motel room in a single bound to knock a hat off a bed. He shares a common rodeo aversion to yellow-colored clothing, too, especially after hanging up on a bronc in his earlier years while riding in a pair of yellow-topped boots.

Joel Edmondson, the 1983 champion bulldogger, was a student of mine here at Emporia State University in the mid-1970s. He also rode bareback broncs back then and was a one-man intercollegiate rodeo team for us. I ran into Joel last May when I was poking around the Flint Hills near Eureka. He had just gotten married to a Eureka girl (she's a real good driver, he said—a major consideration to someone who has to pull a dogging horse fifty-thousand miles a year) and was getting ready to try out a couple of new practice steers, so I went along to watch. Unfortunately, Joel won't be repeating as champion this year. He was hurt in a plane wreck last August. Not seriously, but enough to slow him down for awhile.

I know Sonny Worrell, the 1978 regular-season steer-roping winner (i.e., PRCA champion), slightly. I remember seeing him throw the shot for Fredonia in high school track meets back in the 1950s, and he was picking up broncs for the Flying A Rodeo Company in 1961, the same year I worked as chute help for them. That was the year that Sonny won the calf roping and the all-around title at Cheyenne. He is the son-in-law of the late Everett Shaw, one of the all-time great steer ropers, and his own son Neil is now competing.

The other Kansas champions I do not know so well. I've met Butch Myers (of Welda), the 1980 steer-wrestling champion, a time or two, but I've never met Dave Brock (originally of Goodland), the 1978 calf-roping champion. Butch went into the national finals trailing by several thousand dollars, but put on a great finish to win the title by nearly three thousand. Dave ended the regular 1978 season in eighth place, but won the national finals and the world championship (the only time that system worked to a Kansan's advantage).

The two remaining champions were, I think, the greatest of the lot, if for no other reason than that they were in their prime when I was growing up and thus were nearly mythic heroes to me. I'm talking about Ken and Gerald Roberts of Strong City, home of the Flint Hills Rodeo, which they helped to found back in the mid-1930s. The Roberts family is undoubtedly the premier rodeo family in Kansas. Emmett, the father, is in his nineties and still raises horses on his ranch just east of the rodeo grounds in Strong City. A daughter, Marge (see chapter 18), won the women's bronc riding championship at Cheyenne in 1940; she also claimed to have taught her brothers how to ride. She and Ken are dead now, but Gerald makes chaps and other gear in his western store at Abilene.

Ken is considered by many to be the best natural bull rider of all time. He won three consecutive titles (1943–45) before concentrating on producing rodeos instead of just competing in them. His riding abilities are legendary. Once, for instance, his bull rope is said to have broken, yet he managed to finish the ride with just the grip of his legs. Ask any bull rider how hard that would be!

Gerald is the only all-around champion to come from Kansas, winning the title in both 1942 and 1948. He also came close to winning titles in bull riding and saddle-bronc riding. To a young boy growing up in the Flint Hills, Gerald Roberts was the epitome of the rodeo cowboy—handsome, daring, skilled, devil-may-care. At least that was the reputation that filtered down to a twelve-year-old. I remember hearing some of the older cowboys say that Gerald would hit town with twenty dollars in his pocket (and that was for entry fees), take a room in the best hotel, party all night (buying for everyone), then go out and win two or three events, pay his bills, and head on down the road. Ah, the good old days— before rodeo became family recreation with its own chapter of the Fellowship of Christian Athletes . . .

Beginning with Ken and Gerald Roberts in the early 1940s and continuing through this year with Joel Edmondson, Kansas and Kansans have done well in professional rodeo. Three bull-riding titles, two all-arounds, three saddle-bronc crowns, two steer-wrestling champs, and one steer-roping and one calf-roping title. Tied for fifth in the nation in number of world-champion rodeo cowboys. Take that, you big-hatted Rocky Mountain phonies!

Postscript

Fred Beeson was elected posthumously to the Rodeo Hall of Fame in 1991. He won the first calf roping ever held at Cheyenne and also the steer roping there in 1928. Emmett Roberts died in the spring of 1993 at age ninety-seven. His funeral, held in the rodeo arena at Strong City, was attended by hundreds, including several world champions. Since the above was written, no new Kansas cowboys have won championships, and some new winners have added to the totals of other states. Lewis Feild, for instance, has finally given Utah a champion. But Kansas still ranks high among producers of world-champion rodeo cowboys.

3.   Snick Harrison and the Wallace Rodeo

IN MY younger days the Wallace Rodeo had a certain cachet for me, partly because of its reputation (many of the older rodeo cowboys I was coming into contact with at that time had good things to say about it), partly because of its remoteness (Wallace is way out on the High Plains, about as far as you can go from the Flint Hills and still be in Kansas). The only time I ever rode there, back in the early 1960s, I even won some of the bronc riding. A quarter of a century later I returned to Wallace County to give some folklore programs, and my hosts arranged for me not only to attend the rodeo but to talk with one of the men who started it.

Forrest "Snick" Harrison (his uncle used to call him Snickelfritz) was born in 1922, his brother George in 1920. They started riding at an early age, breaking their father's work horses to ride when they were only nine and eleven years old, then going on as they got older to break horses for neighbors. "We didn't do much walking," Snick told me. "Dad always said that we'd walk a half a mile to catch a horse so we could ride a quarter."

The two brothers had been ranching together for several years, occasionally relieving the tensions of earning a living with a little rodeoing (Snick rode bulls; his brother dogged steers), when they decided to keep some of the bull calves from their herd of Brahma cows, grow them up to riding size, and start putting on rodeos. They began at their hometown in 1954, helping to build the chutes and putting up snow fence for an arena. From there they branched out, producing rodeos for the next half-dozen years in towns throughout western Kansas and eastern Colorado—Oakley, Colby, Leoti, Lakin, Syracuse, Tribune, Sharon Springs, Goodland, Jetmore, Hugo, Brush.

In addition to raising their own Brahma roping calves and bucking bulls, the Harrisons began to build up a good string of bucking horses. "Back in that time you could buy a lot of horses for ten to twenty-five dollars a head. If they wouldn't buck, we'd send them on up to the horse sale at Benkelman, Nebraska, and at least get our money back out of them." A lot of them did buck, however, including a bareback bronc that they bought from Sharon Springs rancher Chuck Singer. They called him Chucker, and he has lived up to his name over a long and successful career. Joanne, Snick's wife, told me that a few years ago, at a ripe old age, Chucker was named the Nebraska bucking horse of the year.

Joanne and her sister-in-law, Doris, kept books and ran the stopwatches, while Snick filled the chutes and George pulled flanks and directed the activity in the arena. Other friends and in-laws hired on to pick up broncs, work chutes, and drive trucks. One of the hazards of rodeo in the 1950s, before some towns built good pens, was having stock jump over the snow-fence arenas. One night at Hugo, Colorado, one of their crossbred Brahma bulls (out of George's Jersey milk cow) jumped the fence, ran through some carnival tents, and disappeared into the dark. Next day, after several hours of searching by car and horseback, they finally spotted the missing bull from an airplane.

What about mishaps and injuries to the cowboys? I asked. Snick said that one of the worst occurred at their practice arena on a Sunday afternoon try-out of new broncs. One of the local first-time bareback riders panicked and failed to bail off when a young palomino mare leaped over the arena fence. Or tried to. She caught her hooves and did a flip. "That kid will never be any deader when he dies," Snick said, "but after they hauled him off to Goodland in an ambulance he came out of it just fine."

In 1960 the Harrison brothers sold their stock and their contracts to the Hudson family of Leoti (Dion Hudson now lives in Sharon Springs and has kept the business going), deciding that what had started out as fun was beginning to seem more like work. "We made a little money with it," Snick said, "but we didn't really care; we just liked doing it." That's the attitude that has kept rodeo going for over a hundred years.

4. *Reb Russell, A Reel Kansas Cowboy*

I DON'T believe that Kansas has produced any world-class cowboy movie stars, a circumstance that doesn't bother me much, to tell the truth, considering the authenticity gap that

exists between movie cowboys and ranch cowboys. In my earlier years I went through the daydreaming stage of hero-
worshipping such screen stalwarts as Tim Holt and Gene
Autry and Lash Larue, but the obvious differences between
the Saturday serials and real ranch work in the Flint Hills
soon had me scoffing at the would-bes on the screen. I just
couldn't have much confidence in cowboys who didn't have
sense enough to drive cattle at a walk instead of a run, who
couldn't tell a gelding from a mare, who bounced all over the
saddle when their horses moved out of a walk. And how could
they ride their horses at a constant run without windbreaking
them? A lariat held wrong bothered me much more than six-
shooters that fired twenty times without reloading.

Undoubtedly I picked this trait up from my father and my
uncle, neither of whom ever had a whole lot of sympathy for a
would-be cowboy, particularly if he had a pretentious air about
him. Maybe that's why I could never understand America's
fascination with John Wayne. He didn't look like a cowboy, he
didn't talk like a cowboy, and he certainly didn't walk like a
cowboy, taking big lumbering strides in clunky old boots instead of the short, choppy steps of a horseman. He couldn't
ride a horse with any kind of grace, either, but then what could
be expected from an Iowegian? Montanan Gary Cooper—
tough as nails but soft-spoken, occasionally self-conscious but
never self-important—now there's a real Man of the West.

Where does Kansas fit into all of this? Well, I have read
somewhere that William S. Hart and Tom Mix worked for a
while on Kansas ranches, and I do know that rodeo-competi-
tors-turned-movie-stars such as Hoot Gibson, Yakima Canutt,
and Will Rogers appeared in Kansas rodeos at one time or
another. Then there was Emmett Dalton, of the infamous
Coffeyville bandit brothers, who spent his final years in California befriending Tom Mix and dabbling in the movie business. Although better known for its outlaws, Coffeyville was
also home to our state's only cowboy movie star (at least the
only one I've been able to learn of): Reb Russell.

Lafayette H. Russell was born May 31, 1905, in Osawat-
omie and died on March 16, 1978, in Coffeyville, where his

family had moved when he was two years old. Those who were growing up in the 1930s may have seen some of Russell's dozen or so films (1932–34), most of them B-Westerns produced by Willis Kent. Football trivia buffs may remember Russell as an All-American from Northwestern and as one of the original Philadelphia Eagles in that team's first year of existence. Many farmers and ranchers in southeastern Kansas (he lived in Coffeyville) and northeastern Oklahoma (his 2,500 acre ranch was just below the border in Nowata County) remember Russell for his innovative Hi-Goal Agriculture, a plan to help small farmers increase productivity and profits without government aid. Voters in the Fifth Congressional District may remember his campaign against Joe Skubitz in 1964. (He lost; no Democrat has ever done well in that district, not even one advocating self-reliance among farmers and ranchers.) Russell was even a circus star for a couple of years after he quit Hollywood.

I never met Reb Russell, but I was at K-State with his foster son (and nephew), Jim, in the early 1960s. A few years ago Jim was displaying some of his dad's memorabilia at Butler County Community College's "Excursions into History" (the theme that year—1984—was the Great American Cowboy), and I got to see my first Reb Russell film, which happened to be *The Man from Hell*. Now some ungenerous critics might say that the title describes the level of acting in this movie; Russell seems awfully stiff and uncomfortable. It was, however, both his first Western and his first starring role, and Russell himself never claimed to be an actor: "They found out I could get on and off a horse, so I made some Westerns," was his assessment of his career. Reb got a little better in his later films. As Jim once told me, "At first he was trying to play something else instead of letting his own personality come out. If he would have kept going and they would have let him be just Reb Russell, he might have made it big."

This belief is seconded by Betty Hedrick, a former teacher at both the high school and the community college in Coffeyville who has expended more than a little effort studying Reb's career. She first met him when she was teaching in a rural Oklahoma school that bordered Reb's ranch. He would occasionally ride by the schoolyard on his horse at recess time: "The kids were drawn to him like the Pied Piper," she told me. Betty believes that if he had stayed with the movies he not only would have been one of the more successful cowboy stars, but could have become a major personality-type star (such as Burt Reynolds or James Garner).

Western film critic Buck Rainey concurs, noting in his book *Saddle Aces of the Cinema* that Russell was a bit modest about his own potential as a film star: "He was a perfect physical specimen; and he was good-looking and already had a name as a football great." Rainey further points out that Russell was under serious consideration by Columbia as a replacement for Ken Maynard—and being promoted by his friend Tom Mix—until Maynard finally came to terms with the studio.

Mix had first met Russell in 1932 when Reb and thirteen other football stars were brought out to Hollywood by Universal Studios to make *The All-American*. Russell had been named All Big Six quarterback when he played for Nebraska in 1928. He also made "Ripley's Believe It or Not" that year for having averaged six yards each time he carried the ball. Reb (he acquired the nickname—which he later adopted as his legal name—while attending Missouri Military Academy) didn't particularly like quarterbacking, however, so he transferred to Northwestern, where, after laying out a year to meet eligibility requirements, he became an All-American fullback. Following one especially tough game against Notre Dame in 1930, in which Reb lacked only four or five yards of gaining as much ground as the entire Notre Dame team, Knute Rockne labeled him "the greatest plunging fullback I have ever seen."

His senior year at Northwestern could well have been the plot of a movie. While diving for a fumble in the season-opener, Russell was kneed in the back and suffered several broken ribs and some fractured vertebrae. He had to sit out most of the rest of the season, but he did get a chance (once he convinced the doctors to cut him out of his body cast three weeks early) to play in the last game of the season. His daughter Betty (now Mrs. Bob Simpson of Tulsa), then five years old, got to see that game. She remembers being given a purple balloon (as were all Northwestern fans) to release into the air after the first home-team touchdown, but because the game was scoreless well into the fourth quarter, she let the gas out of her balloon so that she could keep it for a souvenir. Then Reb, held out because of his injury, was put into the game late in the fourth quarter and scored the only touchdown of the day. Betty remembers crying because she couldn't release her balloon along with the thousands of others that filled the sky.

Reb also played in that season's East-West Shrine Game, held in San Francisco on New Year's Day, 1932, in which he not only led the East to a 7–0 victory but also gained more yards than the entire West team.

After filming *The All-American,* Russell appeared in a serial, *The Lost Special,* and a dog movie, *Fighting to Live.* Then began his string of Westerns, which included titles such as *Outlaw Rule, Arizona Badman, Cheyenne Tornado, Lightning Triggers,* and *Blazing Guns.* Shooting time was about ten days per film, and his co-workers included such people as Gabby Hayes, Andy Devine, Richard Arlen, Yakima Canutt, Lucille Lund, and Smiley Burnette.

Although he was offered a new contract, Russell left Hollywood after the Kent series ended. His Hollywood career may not have been a spectacular one, but Reb does deserve a footnote in cinema history: one of his films (Jim thinks it is *Border Vengeance*) contains an innovative bit of cinematography. Reb was hanged in that movie, a very realistically enacted scene complete with choking, gasping, kicking, and jerking. The censor (or whoever was in charge of such things in 1934) thought it too realistic, so the movie was recalled after release and the scene reshot, this time showing only the shadow of the hanging body, supposedly the first use ever of this eerily effective silhouette technique.

Betty Hedrick says that, considering the crude equipment and working conditions, Reb's movies were not sloppily made. Reb's stuntman (and friend) was Oscar-winner Yakima Canutt, a former rodeo rider who became arguably the best in the business. One of Canutt's most spectacular and difficult feats involved crawling under the horses on a runaway stagecoach, then dropping to the ground, grabbing the back of the coach, and swinging up on it, a scene he performed as John Wayne's double in *Stagecoach*. The stunt was first used, however, with a two-horse spring wagon in one of Reb's movies.

Right after leaving Hollywood, a proposed radio deal that would have put him in competition with "The Lone Ranger" fell through, so Reb joined the Russell Brothers Circus (no relation) with a bullwhip, fancy-shooting, and trick-riding act. He was an excellent trick rider, despite his size (over six feet tall and around two hundred pounds) and his bad back. The following season (1937) he performed with the Downie Brothers Circus, bringing with him a "Congress of Indians," probably hired through his friend Pawnee Bill. Reb was especially adept with the bullwhip. His daughter Betty (then eleven) occasionally acted as his assistant, holding a strip of paper in her mouth while her father, mounted on Rebel (he claimed to be the only whip artist to do this stunt from horseback), would snap it in two, scant inches from her lips— and her eyes. He never missed.

A boy could have worse heroes. Reb Russell might have had a forceful personality ("We were like two bulls in the same pen together," is the way Jim recalls his relationship with Reb), but he embodied some admirable qualities—hard work, concern for others, devotion to his wife and family. Besides that, he knew what he was doing when he got on a horse, whether in the movies or on his ranch. Reb Russell passes the Hoy test of authenticity.

5.   Henry Mudge, Rancher without Peer

IT IS a known fact that cowboys work for a few dollars a day while cattle owners (or traders or commission men) drive Cadillacs and Lincoln Continentals. This fact of economic superiority, however, has never interfered with the working cowboy's innate, God-given surety that he knows a hell of a lot more about the ranching business—how to handle cattle, how to cull cows, how to bring out the best in a good cow horse, how to pick good bulls—than any wheeling-dealing rich rancher ever did.

It doesn't take much reinforcement to confirm such high self-esteem into a firm prejudice, and Henry Mudge was the kind of rancher who has kept western Kansas cowboys smug for over a century.

I first heard of this transplanted Harvard man, heir to a Massachusetts manufacturing fortune, while teaching a folklore workshop at the Santa Fe Trail Center near Larned a few summers back. We were talking about local legends and how town characters sometimes acquire legendary characteristics when one of the students asked if I had ever visited the Mudge ranch, a few portions of which apparently still are visible between Larned and Jetmore. I hadn't, but I did acquire a curiosity-whetting earful of stories about this eccentric early Kansas rancher.

Sometime in 1878 (or 1879 or 1880—accounts in the Kansas State Historical Society vary) Henry Mudge detrained in Larned, accompanied by a pretty girl, who was assumed (falsely, as it turned out) to be Mrs. Mudge, and a male companion (Gus Yesogee), who was introduced as a financial advisor. Yesogee's first bit of advice seems to have been that Larned houses were too small, for Mudge immediately rented two of them—one for entertaining and one for sleeping.

By 1884 Mudge had title to or control over some ten thousand acres and had built a nine-room, L-shaped house, including a "dead room" added on when someone asked Mudge what he would do if there were a death on the ranch and the undertaker couldn't get there. This was not an idle question, for the possibility of accidental death was high, even though there seem never to have been even any serious accidents at the ranch. One of Mudge's favorite pastimes with the many Easterners he entertained (lavishly!) was to get everybody drunk and shoot things—wild game, dogs, holes in the wall, whatever was handy. One of his favorite tricks was to smear a drunken guest with chicken blood, then let him wake up and think that he had been wounded. Another was to give a gun to a greenhorn, then have someone pretend (complete with chicken blood) to have been shot by the novice gunhandler.

Besides drinking and shooting, hunting—especially the chasing on horseback of jackrabbits or coyotes, English fashion—was a favorite entertainment for his many guests, who on occasion included European royalty. Dogs were needed for this kind of hunting, and there were always dozens of them around the ranch. Mudge apparently could never resist buying a dog if the owner claimed it would hunt, and since he readily paid good money for any dog offered him, his cash-hungry homesteading neighbors kept him well supplied. He never seemed to hold a grudge against the people who sold him incompetent dogs, but the poor animal, if it wasn't a hunter (and most of them weren't), often ended up as a target during the drunken shooting sprees.

Mudge's entertaining was the talk of the countryside (especially after the disappearance of the original "Mrs. Mudge"), but he had come west to become a rancher and a rancher he became, the likes of which no one in Hodgeman County had ever seen before—or since. In 1884 he is reported to have had 20 domestic horses, 170 range horses, 3 stallions, 400 range cows, 12 milk cows, 13 Durham bulls (6 purebred and 7 "high grade"), 2 Jersey bulls, and 40 Poland China hogs.

His first big purchase, however, had been sheep—three thousand of them sent up from a Texas ranch. Several dozen soon fell prey to coyotes, while almost the entire flock contracted scabies during the fall of 1880, a time when Mudge was on an extended visit back East. No one on the ranch knew what to do, so the sheep grew worse and worse until Mudge came home in December. He immediately ordered the construction of a dipping vat and commenced dipping—in bitterly cold weather that caused the sodden sheep to freeze as soon as they emerged from the dip. So he had a huge bonfire built and he, his hands, and his eastern guests drove sheep around the fire all night. They also fed warm milk to the worst off of the suffering animals until they ran out of milk, at which point rum from Mudge's well-stocked liquor cabinet was substituted. Sixty head of sheep were dead the next morning, all of them smelling of rum.

As if coyotes and mange weren't enough, Mudge himself was responsible for decimating his flock. He didn't have fences and the neighboring homesteaders would complain when their fields and gardens were invaded. Mudge was generous with damages, so it wasn't as if he didn't have the money to build fence. Somewhere along the way he had been told that sheep could be taught to stay within a prescribed area, so he decided to train his to stay on the property. He sighted the boundary line, shot the first sheep to cross this invisible barrier, then instructed his herders to shoot any and all other animals that strayed over it. Local lore has it that some five hundred sheep were "educated" before Mudge gave up the experiment.

Soon afterwards he went out of the sheep business and invested in cattle. His foreman was a Texan who told his boss that it was wasteful to feed cattle in the winter, that they could survive handsomely on their own on the prairie. What was true for the warmer climate of Texas, however, was not necessarily good advice for western Kansas, and many of his cattle died of starvation before Mudge finally relented and let his hands start feeding them. Ironically (and sadly), when spring came so much hay and feed was left over that he had to have it burned to get it out of the way.

The stories go on: of Mudge wrecking a piano in the Longbranch Saloon in Dodge City because it was out of tune when he sat down to play it, of his kicking out hotel windows in Kinsley when they failed to open easily, of his dumping a tableful of china to the floor in another hotel dining room because one of the plates was cracked, of his shooting a black woman homesteader's guinea fowl because they cackled when he was trying to talk to her. In each case he, as was his wont, paid generous damages.

In fact, Mudge was generous to a fault. He paid good

wages that kept food on the table of many of the farmers and laborers in Hodgeman, Edwards, and Pawnee counties and whiskey in the bellies of the cowboys who worked on his ranch. One reporter noted that "not often are riches inherited by a more deserving man, for he does not hoard it."

Indeed he didn't, and by 1885 he was broke. His ranch passed over to a receiver and Mudge left the country— literally. He traveled to Australia, Borneo, Java, Japan, and China, serving for a time as an oarsman on a whaler. In the early 1890s he was in Montana working on a geological survey and hunting. In 1898 he was married in Rhode Island, where he died ten years later at age fifty-five.

Henry Mudge's Kansas ranch may not have survived, but his name is still well known out where Pawnee Creek runs into the Arkansas River. And his legacy lives on every time a cowboy shakes his head in disbelief at his boss's latest livestock faux pas.

6.   *The Saga of Henry Newton Brown*

It seems that every outlaw in the Old West has been celebrated in folk song. Jesse James had several written about him, the first composed just a few hours after his death ("this song was made by Billy Gashade as soon as the news did arrive") at the hands of gang member Robert Ford ("that dirty little coward"). Billy the Kid has also been the subject of several laudatory songs and poems, and scores of books and movies. Cole Younger, William Clarke Quantrill, Sam Bass, Belle Starr—not to mention twentieth-century hoodlums such as Pretty Boy Floyd and Jake and Ralph Fleagle—have all had their exploits preserved in song. There are even songs about nameless outlaws—generic outlaw songs, I call them— both here ("Bury Me Out on the Prairie") and in Canada ("The Dying Outlaw").

But where, oh where is the folk song about a sheriff or a marshal? Doesn't Wild Bill Hickok deserve a song? Wyatt

Earp and his brothers? Bat Masterson? Oh, there is an obscure song or two about lawmen, anonymous lawmen such as "The Texas Rangers," but no real peace-officer ballad. Could it be because the outlaws were more principled about their calling, doing their robbing and shooting forthrightly, whereas many of the Old West's most famous lawmen were little more than hired guns? They would prostitute their talent with a Colt or a Winchester for whoever was paying the most, turning on their erstwhile friends (e.g., Pat Garrett and Billy the Kid) for the reward money. Besides, it was often hard to tell back then, unless you saw the badge, just who was a peace officer and who was an outlaw.

Take the case of Henry Newton Brown, marshal of the wild cow town of Caldwell alongside the Old Chisholm Trail. Caldwell's record for lawman-longevity was not good: in the two years prior to Brown's appointment as deputy city marshal on July 3, 1882, four city officers had been shot to death. Brown's superior, Bat Carr, seems to have been an effective lawman—at least he didn't get killed, and he had kept the peace without having to kill anyone, either—but his quiet manner (he disliked gunplay) didn't square with Brown's proclivities (he had already killed at least three men and was wanted on two murder charges in New Mexico at the time he took the job in Caldwell), and Brown seems to have squeezed Carr out. By December Carr was gone and Henry Brown was the new city marshal.

He did a good job. For nearly a year and a half, amid the saloons, gambling halls, and houses of prostitution teeming with wild and drunken Texas drovers, he maintained a strict decorum. He himself didn't smoke, drink, chew, or gamble. He did, however, carry a gun, something he did not allow anyone else to do within the city limits. Twice in his sixteen months as marshal he used deadly force in the line of duty. His first killing was of Spotted Horse, an Indian who was causing trouble and who refused to give up his gun. The second was of a gambler, Newt Boyce, who also was shot as he reached for his concealed weapon. Apparently Brown's fellow citizens were not upset by his willingness to use extreme measures to keep the peace: on New Year's Day of 1883 they presented him with a brand new gold-mounted Winchester. The inscription read as follows: "Presented to City Marshal H. N. Brown for valuable service rendered the citizens of Caldwell, Kansas. A. M. Colson, Mayor, Dec., 1882." A local newspaper reporting on the presentation ceremony noted that the gift "testifies in a substantial manner [the citizens'] appreciation of a most efficient officer and worthy gentleman."

The year 1883 went smoothly enough for Brown, if not for the two men he had shot and killed in the line of duty. The local newspaper editor called him "cool, courageous and gentlemanly . . . free from the vices supposed to be proper adjuncts to a man occupying his position; he has earned the confidence of our best citizens and the respect of those disposed to consider themselves especially delegated to run border towns." Well, Brown damn well should have been able to clean up the town; he'd had plenty of experience on the other side of the fence.

He had left his Missouri home at age seventeen and headed west, where he took a job as a cowboy on a Colorado ranch. That was in 1874, a year or so before he killed his first man. By then he was cowboying in the Texas Panhandle, but after the killing he felt safer over the line in New Mexico. Bad company awaited him: Billy the Kid. He rode with Billy for several years during the notorious Lincoln County War and helped to ambush and kill Sheriff William Brady and his deputy, George Hindman. By 1878 he and Billy had become horse "traders," picking up mounts for nothing in New Mexico and selling them in Tascosa, Texas. But Brown was nothing if not flexible; within a year he was a Texas deputy sheriff (Oldham County), spending much of his time running down horse thieves. I expect he knew where to find them, all right.

Somehow or other his drifting landed him in Caldwell by 1882, where he again took up the profession of law enforcement. He also took up matrimony. After winning the approval of the better citizens of Caldwell during his first full year as head marshal, he set out to win the affection of

Maude Levagood, daughter of one of Caldwell's foremost families. They were married in March of 1884. The next month, after achieving the distinction of a third consecutive appointment as city marshal (no one else had ever made it for more than a year in the job), Brown bought a house.

So Henry Newton Brown had it all: the respect of the citizens of Caldwell, symbolized by his fancy new rifle; the love of a good woman, symbolized by the bonds of holy matrimony; and a nice, new house to live in, symbolized by a nice fat mortgage. Oh, he had it all, all right, except for enough money to maintain himself and his new wife. His wages were something like fifteen hundred dollars a year, good pay for the times, but the house and furniture and milk cow staked out back had set him back a bundle. He owed the bank over a thousand dollars. Besides, he liked to have plenty of spending money to toss around.

In this situation of economic need his previous experience came in handy. If one needed horses, he had learned in New Mexico, one went to a horse ranch and took them. Therefore, if one needed money, one should simply go where money was to be found—a bank, say—and take some. So he did just that. Or tried to. After enlisting the help of his deputy, a tall Texan possessed of a secretive past named Robertson who went by the name of Ben Wheeler, and a couple of cowboys from the Gypsum Hills, Billy Smith and John Wesley, he rode a hundred miles or so west to the town of Medicine Lodge and robbed the Medicine Valley Bank.

Now some believe that the heist was supposed to have been an inside job, that one of the tellers had been recruited to help and that the bank's president was supposed to have been out of town. But plans had changed, and when Brown and his gang burst into the bank on April 30 they found E. W. Payne, the president, and George Geppert, a clerk, on the job. Payne made a sudden determination to protect his establishment, reaching for his gun as Geppert moved to set the combination on the safe. Both men were shot and killed, but Payne lived long enough to identify Brown as his assailant. The foiled robbers jumped on their horses and headed out into the rugged country southwest of town, where they had fresh horses hidden, but fate, in the form of a recently erected barbed wire fence, headed them into the only box canyon in the entire Gypsum Hills. Sam Denn, marshal of Medicine Lodge, and his posse trapped the fugitives and engaged them in a two-hour gun battle. Their ammunition spent, Brown and his gang surrendered and were taken back to the city jail.

An angry mob (they're always angry when they're getting ready to lynch somebody) gathered around the jail as Brown asked for writing materials. He wrote his new, and innocent, wife a farewell letter, pledging his love and offering instructions for liquidating his estate: "I will send you all of my things, and you can sell them, but keep the Winchester." That evening the mob rushed the jail, overcame the guards, and opened the cell doors, intending to hang the murderers being kept therein. But once free of their chains, the four men made a run for it. Brown was shot and killed, the others caught and hanged from a nearby elm.

I don't know the reaction of Mrs. Brown when she received word of the robbery and its aftermath, but she was undoubtedly as shocked as the rest of Caldwell: the news hit the town like "a thunderbolt at midday," according to a local newspaper. Doubts and denials eventually succumbed to reluctant acknowledgment. Brown's obituary noted that he had been accepted socially by the citizens, a rare occurrence in cow towns, and that he was "a prominent figure at church socials and picnics." Was this only a deceitful ploy on his part, wondered the eulogist, or did it signify a new direction Brown wished his life to take? We'll never know for sure, but it does seem to me that it would have been pretty hard for Brown, back in those days innocent of such things as savings-and-loans scandals, Charles Keating, and Silverado, to have justified his actions as those of a respectable middle-class citizen. No, I think that old duality, that tension between lawman and lawbreaker in the Old West, was a force that Brown just couldn't overcome. He was twenty-seven years old when he died.

And his rifle? How long his widow kept it, if at all, no one knows for sure. It disappeared from sight decades before being acquired by a gun collector in Texas. In 1978 the famous Winchester of the infamous bank-robbing marshal was donated to the Kansas State Historical Society. It can be seen today at the Kansas Museum of History in Topeka.

Part Two

OLD TIMERS

(January 1990)

"OLDEST Cowboy Found Dead Wednesday in Texas Pasture" was the headline on a filler item that brought me up short as I was reading our local paper one day last week. Tom Blasingame was dead. At the time of his death he was working for the JA Ranch, which was started by Charles Goodnight back in the 1880s. I don't know, but most likely the two knew each other: Blasingame was thirty-one when the pioneer cowman died in 1929. But whereas Goodnight was a cowboy who became a big rancher, Blasingame remained a working cowhand all his life.

At the time he was born, at Waxahachie on Groundhog's Day, 1898, there was probably no such thing as a ninety-one-year-old cowboy. The earliest cowboys, who had come into being on the Old Chisholm Trail to Abilene in the years following the Civil War, called themselves drovers. A majority of these early trail hands were said to have been teenage boys, which means that a cowboy in his fifties would have been a grizzled veteran at the turn of the century.

Tom Blasingame was thought to be the oldest working cowboy in Texas (perhaps the country). Not that there aren't other old timers still active to one degree or another in the cattle business. In fact, a couple of weeks ago I visited with Harvey Smith of Burdick, an eighty-three-year-old man who cowboys full time here in the Flint Hills, and I share an office with the nephew of Bill Brown, a Montana rancher who, a couple of years back at age eighty-two, roped over a thousand of his own calves and dragged them to the branding fire just to prove that he could still do it. But Blasingame apparently was working every day at regular cowhand chores. In fact, on the day he died, he had been riding pastures on a colt he was training.

According to the news account, Blasingame had told an interviewer last summer that when his time came, he wanted to die in a pasture. Apparently, that is what he did: "He must have known he was in trouble, dismounted, and just laid down and died. There were no bruises or scratches so he wasn't bucked off," according to ranch manager Johnny Farrar. Blasingame was found lying peacefully on his back, his hands folded on his chest.

Blasingame was famous for more than age; his reputation as a top hand with cattle and horses had, in fact, been celebrated several years ago in an Ian Tyson song. On the other hand, he was not a world-champion rodeo performer or the owner of a huge ranch. His honors (from the National Cowboy Hall of Fame, among others) may have been triggered by age, but they were awarded for being, simply, a good hand. There's no higher honor than that.

I got to meet Tom Blasingame at the National Cowboy Symposium in Lubbock in June 1989. One of the singers had done the Tyson song about him, and later pointed him out to me. After some initial hesitation, I thought, what the hell, and walked up to him and introduced myself. He asked where I was from, and I said Emporia, Kansas. "How are the Flint Hills looking?" he asked. "A little dry this spring," I told him. "Have you been up in our part of the country?" "No," he said, "but we've sent some cattle up there, and I hear the grass is wonderful."

Tom Blasingame appreciated good grass; what better place to lie down for your final sleep.

8. *Melvin Betters, Open-Range Cowboy*

THERE aren't too many old-timers left who rode the open range, but I recently ran across one up at Miltonvale, Kansas. When Melvin Betters (born 1899) was ten, his father moved the family from Miltonvale to Sheridan, Wyoming, where Elma Betters's twin sister, Alma Jones, and her husband lived. "Shoot 'em Up" Jones (he got the nickname from the time he had indulged in a little too much snakebite medicine and took target practice with his .38 Colt on some of the bottles on the shelf behind the bar) was the foreman on the Wrench Ranch near Sheridan, owned by a mogul of the Burlington Railroad. Betters isn't sure just what his farmer father's qualifications for assistant foreman were, other than nepotism, but his father was good at handling the men and he himself loved the chance not just to play cowboy but to be one.

Shortly after the family arrived on the ranch (where Mrs. Betters assisted her sister in cooking for the crew, which during the summer months could run as high as a hundred men), the horse wrangler quit, so young Melvin got the job and the ten dollars a month that went with it. While the men were having breakfast, he would go out to the barn and saddle his horse, then run the rest of the remuda in from the horse pasture. There were several large fenced pastures near ranch headquarters, but during the summer most of the cattle were driven to the open-range country near the Bighorn Mountains, where several different brands were grazed on public land.

Betters got to help with the fall roundup—eating at a chuck wagon, sleeping out on a bedroll, riding night-herd, and associating with gun-carrying cowboys. When I asked about stampedes, he said that he remembered several short runs but only one real stampede. He was helping to move cattle off a military reservation, where artillery practice had been scheduled. They had the cattle out of the danger zone, but when the guns started firing the noise spooked them. They ran off and on for three days and nights, and some of the cattle injured their hooves so badly that they had to be destroyed.

He also recalled one particular drive of sixteen hundred head of longhorn steers, which had been purchased from a ranch forty miles north of Sheridan. Those longhorns could really move. The drive started at four o'clock in the morning and by eleven o'clock that night they not only had brought the cattle onto the Wrench headquarters but had branded all but two of them. Those two had horns too wide to fit the

squeeze chute, so they were roped and branded the next day.
The herd was stretched out for two or three miles, so when
the leaders hit the pens, the branding started. It continued
steadily during the several hours it took for the rest of the
cattle to reach the ranch. Betters's job was to dally the rope
attached to the handle of the squeeze chute onto his saddle
horn, ride forward a couple of steps to tighten it, then back
his horse up when the steer was to be released. The cattle
moved through so efficiently that he wore his horse out and
had to change mounts.

After three years at Sheridan the Betters family moved to a
ranch in western Nebraska, where Melvin put in another
three years as a cowboy. Then his father moved the family
back to the farm at Miltonvale.

Many long-time plainsdwellers I have interviewed over the
years have talked about how hard life on the farm was, how
busy they were doing their chores and helping with the work.
But compared to the hours, the activity, and the excitement
of the range, farm work was easy for Melvin Betters. After all,
he had only half a dozen horses to bring in each morning on
the farm, not six hundred.

9. Ralph Bowlby

RALPH BOWLBY, born in 1889, is a rancher from the breaks of
the Saline River south of Natoma, Kansas. In the fall of 1986
Dean Banker, from Russell, who operates the state's oldest
family-owned clothing store, took me out to the ranch for a
visit with the ninety-seven-year-old Bowlby. Bowlby's reputation for crustiness preceded him. As we drove to the ranch,
for example, Banker told me that a woman in Russell had
wondered why in the world anyone, especially a college pro-
fessor, would want to go talk to "that old drunk." Well, if
there's one thing I've learned as a folklorist, it's that you
don't have to have been a saint to have led a life worth
examining. A man can have a weakness—for the bottle, say—

and still have something interesting to contribute to the store of human knowledge. A good recipe for a hangover, if nothing else—Bowlby's was a half pound of raw hamburger mixed up with raw egg and salt and pepper. You can also learn that deepshaft, the nickname given the top quality bootleg made in southeastern Kansas during Prohibition, brought up to thirty dollars a gallon by the time it had made the trip to Russell County.

It took a bit of doing to find the Bowlby ranch (this is range country with few roads and fewer houses), but after a bit of backtracking and map-checking we drove into the yard of a typical-looking plains farmstead—a two-story frame house, a few outbuildings, native grass lawn, and a few shade trees, trees tall enough to let me know that this site had been occupied for many decades. We were greeted with coffee by Bowlby's wife, the former Angie Acosta, a Peruvian woman who had married Bowlby in Mexico years earlier, and by a small and clever dog performing tricks for us in response to commands in both English and Spanish. Like many another successful Great Plains rancher, Bowlby belies the popular stereotype of plains provincialism with much foreign travel—to Africa, Australia, Central and South America, Mexico.

The artifacts of Bowlby's life and travels fill the house, from the mounted sailfish on a wall in the living room to the Dutch oven on the buffet in the dining room (a utensil used in roundups on the Bowlby ranch in earlier years) to the eclectic collection of western and South Americana hanging from hooks on the back porch—arrows and spears and bolos and horse-hair bridles and rawhide lariat ropes and Winchesters and bison horns and Mexican spurs with huge rowels. Most telling of all, I thought, was a photographic portrait of a mounted man, an enlargement yellowing with age and displayed in an ornate oval frame. This type of portrait was popular with our grandparents around the turn of the century, but Bowlby himself is the subject in this picture.

One of the great pleasures of studying the history and folklore of cowboys is having the opportunity to talk with old-timers like Bowlby, to hear firsthand accounts of polo and

early rodeo and barn dances (with jugs of moonshine hidden
in the woodpile) and cattle-working and horse-breaking.
Back in the 1920s, for instance, Bowlby and his friends would
ride thirty or forty miles to Hays for Sunday afternoon polo
games, leading their playing ponies to keep them fresh, then
ride home again when the matches were over.

Bowlby is one of those cowboys whose exploits have in-
spired tales and legends. My favorite is about the time some
twenty-five years ago when a neighbor's bull got into a pasture of Bowlby heifers. After the hired man put him out a few
times, Bowlby went to the owner's house to warn him to keep
the bull away, saying that he didn't want the heifers bred and
would take steps to insure the bull's inability to breed anything if he got back in the pasture. Oh, no, said the owner,
you wouldn't do that—he's worth X-thousands of dollars.
Then keep him out of my pasture, was the response.

A couple of days later Bowlby and his hired man were
checking the heifer pasture when, sure enough, they spotted
the bull. Bowlby, who was in his seventies at the time, put the
hired man behind the wheel while he himself stood in the
back of the pickup and roped the bull. Then he tied him to
the bumper, took out his Case knife, and, as my father might
say, made a gentleman of the trespassing bovine. He next
drove to the neighbor's house, leading the newly docile ex-
bull behind the pickup. Turning him loose in the yard,
Bowlby knocked on the door and told the astonished owner,
"Here's your steer." The following day every neighbor with a
bordering pasture (and there were many because the Bowlby
land holdings were extensive) was out checking fence.

At age ninety-seven Ralph Bowlby has undoubtedly soft-
ened, but he is still a formidable character. Although he
cannot get around now as well as he could a few years back,
he continues to oversee the maintenance of the ranch, including the care of a two hundred–head cow herd. When I
asked him about his favorite horses, he mentioned Missy, a
mare he currently owns. "But I haven't ridden her for two
years," he told me. "It's not as much fun as it used to be."
Maybe not, but he is where he wants to be. In response to a

suggestion that it might be time to leave the ranch and move to town Bowlby replied, "I'd rather be in hell with a broken back than have to live in town!"

Postscript

Ralph Bowlby died on October 4, 1988, just a month shy of his ninety-ninth birthday. Twenty mounted cowboys led the horse-drawn hearse to a hillside two miles north of the ranch house, where Bowlby was buried. Which way he went, and the soundness of his bones, isn't known, but at least he's not living in town.

10. *Shorty Hougland, Cattle Trader*

DURING the years I was growing up, I spent many a Saturday with my father at the livestock auction at El Dorado. Only back then it was called a community sale and people sold any and every thing—household items, produce, chickens, goats— not just cattle and hogs. We usually got there in time for some of the junk (as Dad called it) to sell, but we were primarily interested in the livestock—whether as sellers or buyers or just checking the market. I can still see some of the regulars in my mind's eye—Walt Butterworth and Jim Butts, the auctioneers; Oss Geer, an old-timer who earned a little tobacco money doing odd jobs; Lamar Jones, a trucker from El Dorado; and a man from Latham, Walker I think was his name, who seemed always to have a few cattle to sell—he was a trader, driving the southern Flint Hills to buy a cow here, a couple of steers there, then either selling them to individual farmers or taking them to one of the auctions in the area.

Today that type of cattle trader, if not extinct, is certainly an endangered species, done in largely by the advent of the stock trailer, which allows even small operators to transport their own cattle or hogs easily and cheaply. No more hiring a professional trucker to haul cows to a sale or discounting them on the farm to a trader. Not that there aren't still plenty

of cattle buyers around, but that's just what they are—buyers—
not the old-time livestock trader. Recently, however, I had a
chance to talk to one of the originals, a man who for some
sixty years made his living plying the roads of southeastern
Kansas buying and selling cattle.

William "Shorty" Hougland passed the century mark on
June 22, 1982. When I visited him in a Humboldt nursing
home the day after Christmas 1986 he was just as wiry and
quick as all the stories I had heard about him. Actually, I had
met Shorty briefly nearly twenty-five years earlier when I was
visiting Cathy (this was before we were married) on her parents' dairy farm near Chanute. Shorty, who specialized exclusively in dairy cattle, often stopped by to talk to my father-in-
law, Wilbur Thompson, or his nephew, Britton Thompson,
who dairied nearby.

Shorty had been buying cows from the Thompson herd
since the 1930s, Wilbur told me on the drive up to Humboldt, and he had an uncanny knack for immediately zeroing
in on the best cow in the herd. "How much for that one?" he
would ask repeatedly, ignoring all of Wilbur's attempts to get
him to bid on a heifer he (Wilbur) wanted to cull from the
herd. "You always bought our best cows," Wilbur told Shorty,
a little accusingly, during our visit. "I always tried to," he
fired right back. Shorty, in fact, was regarded by his peers
(dairy farmers, auctioneers, other traders) as the best judge
of dairy cattle in southeastern Kansas.

When we arrived at the Pinecrest Nursing Home, Shorty
(he fit his nickname; he couldn't have been more than five
feet tall) was seated facing the door, an open can of peanuts
on a TV tray in front of him and a package of Redman on the
bed. Some shreds of tobacco lay on the floor around his
chair, but the coffee-can spittoon was unmissed. They hadn't
seen each other for a couple of years, but Shorty knew Wilbur
immediately, although it took him a minute or two to get my
brother-in-law, Craig, straight in his mind. Shorty's hearing is
good and he wears glasses only to read. He likes company
and kept telling us to sit down on the bed until we finally did.

"How many cows are you milking?" he wanted to know.

"Where are you shipping the milk? What did you get for Christmas?" When Wilbur asked him that same last question, Shorty waved to the nearly empty can of honey-roasted peanuts. "What did you have for dinner?" Wilbur asked. "I ain't had no dinner yet," was the quick comeback. "Somebody must be standing on the cook's shirttail."

We found out, however, that he had indeed been served his Christmas dinner, a special one. A little background information about Shorty's tastes might be useful here. In his earlier years he drank, heavily ("only good stuff, none of that bootleg"), and always had a cigar in his mouth. He still chews, but hasn't had a drink for a quarter of a century. Wilbur tells of stopping by the house shortly after Mrs. Hougland died and Shorty pointing out a partly filled pint bottle on a shelf: "I put that there fifteen years ago and I haven't touched a drop since." His choice of high-cholesterol foods, especially raw milk fresh from the Thompson dairy (Britton would usually take Shorty a gallon when he went to visit), does not exactly coincide with AMA recommendations. "He liked bacon and eggs," Wilbur said, detailing Shorty's basic menu and cooking repertoire in the five years between his wife's death and the time he moved into Pinecrest at age one hundred. "By God, I like it yet," Shorty said, "but here they just give you a little smell of bacon all fried away to nothing." (He likes his bacon fat and chewy.) On Christmas morning, though, the Pinecrest staff had served him a whole pound of bacon for breakfast and another of his favorites for dinner: sauerkraut and barbecued ribs. My stomach trembled at the thought, yet there he was the next day eating peanuts and complaining because dinner was late.

Shorty's family moved to Kansas City from Macon, Missouri, when he was around ten years old. After working for a time at the stockyards there, he bought dairy cattle for Kansas City livestock buyer John Horner for ten years, then bought cows for the Shawnee Dairy Cattle Company for an additional seven years.

In the early 1920s he went to Colorado to farm, but between drought and hailstorms he lost everything. Flat broke, he put in with a baker in Holly. Shorty was a willing worker, and for three years he and his partner did well, especially with their promotional gimmick: a silver dollar baked into one out of every hundred loaves of bread. "The women couldn't buy it fast enough," Shorty said. But the baker's wife ordered him around one day (I had the feeling, listening to him tell about the episode, that not many people had ever successfully ordered him around), so Shorty told his partner, "Either I'm going to buy you out or you're going to buy me out." When the negotiations ended at three o'clock the next morning, Shorty was headed back to Kansas. As for Colorado: "I wouldn't give a dime for the whole state."

After his return he did some dairying, but mainly he traded cows. For over sixty years he and his Hudson (the brand of automobile he drove from 1917 until they quit making them) were a familiar and welcome sight to farmers all over southeastern Kansas. "I'd be out trading yet," he said, "but cattle got too high. When any old cow was costing four hundred dollars, I had to quit." That period in the market occurred when Shorty was nearing ninety years of age.

Wilbur tells of the time a few years after that, at just about the peak of the dairy market, when Shorty, recently a widower, phoned about buying some heifers. Wilbur said he didn't have any to sell. Shorty, not to be put off, asked, "What about Craig?" Wilbur allowed that Craig did have a few springers, pretty good first-calf heifers. "How much would he want for them?" Shorty wanted to know. "I really couldn't say," Wilbur stalled. "How much?" Shorty demanded. "Well, I think Craig can probably get eight hundred fifty or nine hundred dollars a head for them," Wilbur said. There was silence on the other end of the phone. A long silence. Then Shorty's crackling voice: "Are you standing on a chair?" Shorty never bought any cattle after that.

Shorty Hougland not only typifies the livestock trader I remember from my youth (even though he specialized in dairy cattle rather than dealing in all breeds), but he also embodies what I think is a hallmark of the spirit here in the tallgrass prairie region—through honest effort he made a

good life, a steady life, for himself and his family in the face
of adversity, and he wasn't plagued by delusions of grandeur.
He was content to trade a couple of cows here, a few more
there; success was in doing what he did well, not in being the
world's biggest cattle dealer. "I've had a lot of fun in my life.
That's what you live for," he said as we were leaving. "Can I
bring you anything?" Wilbur asked at the door. "Yes, a thousand dollars," was the reply.

"I guess Shorty's slowing down," Wilbur said as we got
into the pickup and drove away. "He always used to ask for a
million."

Postscript

Shorty Hougland died in the spring of 1987, a few weeks
short of his one hundred fifth birthday.

11. *Lee Carter*

IN TERMS of population Wallace County is just about the
smallest in Kansas, its two thousand or so citizens placing it
only a couple of hundred ahead of Greeley, its southern
neighbor on the far western border of the state. But population density isn't always a good measure of what a region has
accomplished, and in terms of history and interesting people
Wallace is one of the top counties on the Great Plains. Butter-
field Overland Dispatch stagecoaches once rolled along the
Smoky Hill Trail on their way from Atchison and Leavenworth to Denver. Indian braves once challenged the soldiers
stationed at Fort Wallace, whose cavalrymen rescued their
besieged fellow troopers at Beecher's Island just across the
Colorado border in the fight where the great Cheyenne war-
rior Roman Nose was killed.

During the past several years I've had a few chances to
spend time in the shortgrass of Wallace County, and I couldn't
have been treated any nicer. One thing my hosts did, knowing of my interest in history and folklore, was arrange for me

to visit with several of the old-timers out there. And whether it's the clear air, the clean living, or the hard work, more than a few people out in that country get to be old-timers.

One particularly interesting man I met was Lee Carter, who was ninety-one when I first talked to him in 1986. In his younger days Carter had helped to drive cattle in herds of a thousand head and more from New Mexico to Kansas. This was pretty late, about the time of World War I, so trains were certainly available, but apparently it was cheaper to drive the cattle than to haul them. A number of ranchers from Wallace County would buy New Mexico cattle each spring, then send a trail crew, usually bossed by Al Beam, to Clayton to pick them up. For several years young Lee Carter was one of the cowboys who helped drive them up what they called the Cimarron Trail to Holly, Colorado, and then northeast to Wallace. In the fall the cattle would be loaded onto Union Pacific cars and shipped to the stockyards in Kansas City.

In late 1917 Carter joined the U.S. Navy and was stationed in Chicago. Unable to get into a radio technology unit, he parlayed his experience as cornetist with his hometown cowboy band into a position with the Navy band, which at the time happened to be under the directorship of John Philip Sousa. After his discharge in 1919, he hired on with Ringling Brothers and toured the country with the circus band for a few months, but he soon tired of the life of a traveling musician and returned to Wallace County. He still enjoyed travel, however, and through the years he managed to visit many of the states, as well as Great Britain, Ireland, Europe, Israel, Canada, and Brazil, where he took a float trip down the Amazon.

From 1920 to 1930 Carter had a hardware store in Weskan before moving to Sharon Springs and running a filling station for a couple of years. In 1932 he started the Carter Coal, Feed, Hardware, Lumber, and Gasoline Company, which he ran until his retirement in 1960. He also told me something I didn't know whether to believe or not—that hogs like coal. One farmer would buy all Carter's slack coal and dump it into a stock car with his market hogs. By the time the train

got to Kansas City, the cheap coal was in pig stomachs, ready
to be weighed up at higher hog-market prices.

At one point I asked Carter about his birthplace. "I was
born in a sod house here in Wallace County," he replied,
"lived here in Wallace County, and I'll die and be buried
beneath Wallace County sod, I guess." That prediction came
true in the summer of 1989, bringing to an end a long and
colorful life.

12.   *Waldo Hoss and Rattlesnakes*

WALDO HOSS. Even Larry McMurtry couldn't come up with a
better name for a wizened, leather-tough, old-time cowboy.
But Waldo isn't fictional. He's from the High Plains of Kansas, one of the several Wallace Countians I've had the chance
to visit with in the past few years. He still lives on the place
where he was born, the homestead his father settled in 1902,
seven years before Waldo's birth. He attended a one-room
school with the children of black homesteaders who lived in
the neighborhood, but quit school after the eighth grade and
began riding for some of the neighboring ranchers. He was
barely in his teens when he leased some land himself and
bought a few cattle of his own to run.

Yes, Waldo Hoss knows cattle and he knows horses. He
ought to. Not only did he ride horses while looking after
cattle, but he broke scores of teams of horses and mules for
farm work. And he may well have been the last man on the
plains to buy a car. In 1953. At age forty-four. Not till then did
Hoss finally break down and buy a pickup, a 1948 Dodge.
Why did he wait so long, I asked. "I don't know," he replied.
"I just always rode a horse and I always said that was the
biggest mistake I ever made when I bought that automobile."
Not that he didn't know how to drive: "You see, I'd drove
about three cars before that, because I worked for farmers
and ranchers who had them." But his horse continued to be

his chief mode of transportation for several years even after he bought the car.

In the late 1930s Hoss got a chance to relive a little history—the open-range days. He was working for a man who had leased or bought an old ranch that had been abandoned for several years during the drought. In the summer they received thirty-three hundred head of horned Mexican cattle that had to be herded because the fences had all deteriorated. So the cowboys would build fence by day, then take turns riding night-herd. Except, he said, for some of the younger hands who got scared out. This ranch was near the old Fort Wallace cemetery, and sometimes the night herders would spook themselves, thinking they were seeing the ghosts of ancient troopers and Indians. Then they would come to the bunkhouse and some of the older hands would have to finish the night-herding.

On occasion Hoss worked for the Robidoux Ranch, one of the largest in the area. It bordered the Hoss homestead several miles north of Wallace, and he remembers once, as a kid, helping Pete Robidoux drive some horses. They rode from the ranch into Wallace to stay the night with Pete's mother, then the next day rode clear to Leoti, some forty miles away, to gather horses. "Mr. Robidoux run land that far away back then," Hoss said.

The Robidouxes were a pioneer merchant family with roots in St. Joseph, Missouri, and they established, in Wallace, the biggest general merchandise store between their Missouri headquarters and Denver. Hoss remembers well the store and the story of its closing, how one day not a single customer had come in by noon, so Robidoux locked the door and never opened it again. For years it stood, shelves full. Occasionally a family member would go in for something, but it was never again open to the public.

Somehow or other the subject turned from ranches and the Robidouxes to rattlesnakes. Hoss no longer owns a cow herd and for the past few years he has been pasturing steers in the summer on his own and on leased land. He mentioned that rattlesnakes used to be thick, but that in the previous summer (1987) he had killed only two. "In all the pastures I was through, only two rattlers. Used to be nothing to see three or four every day when I was out in the pasture. And I never had anything rattlesnake bit last summer. That's the first time." Ordinarily, he said, every summer he'd see at least one horse or cow with a swollen leg or jaw.

I asked if he'd ever been bitten. "I've been lucky, I guess," he replied. "I've had them go right through my arms when I was shocking wheat. A loose bundle, or one too heavy to pick up by the string, I'd put my arms around it to gather it up and I just gathered the snake up, too. But they just crawled right on out and never bit me."

Another time Hoss was out with his wife and son fixing an electric fence. The wind was blowing, and he was down on one knee trying to get the wire threaded through an insulator when, "I thought I felt something hitting me on the pants leg. I looked and there was a rattlesnake's tail hitting me on my boot. I had my knee right on his head." He probably should have kept it there while he dispatched the snake, but reflexes don't always do the sensible thing. But when he jerked back, letting the snake free, "he just took off."

I remember my Aunt Virginia telling of running down into the storm cave to get some canned goods for dinner, then being afraid to come back out because there was a bull snake on one of the steps. Something similar happened to Hoss, only it was a four-foot prairie rattler. His grandmother was feeding threshers and sent young Waldo to get a dish out of a cupboard in a room at the back of the house. This room was actually a cellar of sorts that adjoined the house, the place where the family separated cream, made butter, and kept eggs and vegetables. The sort of place, in other words, that a snake really loves on a blistering hot High Plains day.

"When I jerked that cupboard door open," Hoss told me, "there was an old rattler, just a-laying full length. Well, I knew better than to holler because that whole herd of threshers might panic. So I called to my uncle, 'Come here, Dutch.' He came in and when he saw the snake on that shelf, he shut the door to the house so they couldn't hear us in there. Then he said, 'You're going to have to get ahold of him to get him off of there.' The only thing he could find right quick that he thought he could kill him with was one of them stirrers that you stir cream with in a ten-gallon can. He unhooked that and I grabbed the snake by the tail and jerked him off of the shelf down onto the cement floor and Dutch kept a-moppin' at him till he got him. He was huge."

"Weren't you scared to grab him by the tail that way?" I asked. "Yeah," he replied, "but I knew that was the only thing I could do. Now, if I'd had a glove it wouldn't have bothered me as much." It would have bothered me, I can tell you, even if I had been wearing elbow-length medieval chain-mail gauntlets. In fact, if I had been doing the snake killing that day, both the butter paddle and the cupboard would have been kindling by the time it was all over.

13.   *Carl Durgeloh, Baseball Player*

CARL DURGELOH was born on a farm near Sharon Springs, Kansas, in 1897. When he was a boy, his family moved into town, where his father opened a butcher shop; there were enough workers at the Union Pacific roundhouse to support two such establishments back in those days. He remembers one year when his father ground up seven hundred pounds of hamburger for just one community celebration. Durgeloh still lives in Sharon Springs, but his fondest memories are about baseball and rodeos and hunting, not cutting meat.

Durgeloh didn't compete in rodeos, but he did perform as a clown. Back in those days there weren't any bulls for a clown to fight—cowboys rode cows or steers—so what did a rodeo clown do? "I Indian clowned for 'em," he told me, and when I asked what that meant he said, "I made a black cap, hoodlike, with long braided hair and a headdress, and I'd clown around out in the arena. If a guy would tie a calf, I would grab it by the tail when they let it up and go a ways with it. Just clown around."

Hunting was something he didn't clown around about, especially when an oyster supper lay in the balance. Some of the young men would form teams, about a dozen on each side, and go out for a specified time period in search of pests—prairie dogs, hawks, coyotes, cottontails, jackrabbits— with so many points awarded for each kind of animal. The losing team had to foot the bill for an oyster supper for the winners. And also for an orchestra, because they always followed the supper with a dance. "One night we danced practically all night," Durgeloh recalled.

To hear him talk now, it's easy to see that Carl Durgeloh's real passion was baseball. He played center field for Sharon Springs. Were you a hitter? I asked him. "Not very good," he replied. "Oh, I hit fair, but not very good. I could run awful fast, that was one thing." Speed was important because only one team, Tribune, had a fenced ball park. In the other towns, no matter how hard the ball was hit, if the fielder was fast enough he could rob any hitter of a home run. "Were the games exciting?" I asked. "Oh Lord yes!" was the response. "And who were the opponents?" "We had a league right around here," he said. "Weskan had a team, and Winona, Tribune, Leoti, and Oakley. Cheyenne Wells over in Colorado. We had a tournament here every year." "How did your team do?" I asked. "We won it every year."

He also recalled touring professional teams that came out west: bearded Jewish players on the House of David team, black players (including Satchel Paige) on the Kansas City Monarchs. Sharon Springs and the other local teams, however, were not entirely uncorrupted by professionalism. "Everybody would spike up their team, especially for the tournaments," Durgeloh said. That is, he explained, they would bring in a ringer or two. Sharon Springs, for instance, had a left-handed pitcher, Claude Richardson, who threw such a wicked curve that they had to bring in a catcher from Kansas City to catch him. "Big Dell" (the only name Durgeloh remembered him by) would come out on the train on Friday for the weekend games, then go back on Monday. Richardson was good enough that St. Louis tried to sign him up,

but he didn't want to give up the security of his job with the
Union Pacific.

The popularity of baseball began to diminish in the 1930s,
Durgeloh told me. "I don't know why—it just faded away
like." Carl Durgeloh hasn't faded away, though, and neither
have his memories of the glory days of his youth.

14. *Mike Nealis*

ANOTHER Wallace County old-timer I met and got to talk with
back in 1986 was Mike Nealis, a forthright man who had lived
through wind, drought, dust storms, grasshoppers, and jackrabbits. He was ninety-one at the time, some three years before his death. His family had moved from the tallgrass of
Wamego in the Flint Hills to the shortgrass of the High Plains
when he was ten, and he pointed out a huge old cottonwood
tree that was on the place when he arrived. "Indians camped
under that tree in '87," he said. "It was pretty big even back
then."

I asked what was the country like then. "Well, it was a
pretty damn dreary place," Nealis responded. "Now watch
your language," Mrs. Nealis said with a laugh, knowing, I
think, what his response would be. "Hell, that's natural language to me. All them old guys I was around growing up
swore like troopers. My dad and mother didn't allow it, but
that didn't stop us. I picked it up, all right."

One of the places he picked it up was the hay field. The
creek valley his ranch is in is good alfalfa ground, and Nealis
recalled helping his father bale hay, using a "sweep rake"
(what I would call a go-devil, and what others sometimes
term a buck rake or a hay buck) and an Autofadan stationary
baler. Young Mike's job was to thread wires, while his father
and other men would pitch hay into the baler as it was
dumped. Horses moving in a circle powered the machine,
and when they got tired, Nealis said, "That's when you learned

how to swear right damn good." Baled hay would be trans-
ported for sale, while hay for local cattle was fed from stacks.
What was left in the stacks after the jackrabbits, that is.
"They would pretty near eat that deep and that high right
around the alfalfa stacks," he told me, gesturing with hands
spread far apart. Nealis didn't participate in too many rabbit
drives, but he recalled a small one east of Wallace that netted
over four thousand. Another time he was hauling feed to his
cattle when he heard a roar of constant gunfire. Rabbit hunt-
ers were firing so much that their guns literally got too hot to
hold. "Where are all the jacks?" I asked, knowing that you
might drive from the Texas to the Nebraska panhandles today without seeing a single jackrabbit. Part of the reason, he
thinks, is that more ground is broken out, and part can be
blamed on all the spraying of insecticides and herbicides.

Nealis cowboyed a lot in his younger days, helping to drive
herds of cattle (five hundred to a drove) from Lamar, Colorado,
to Sharon Springs as late as the 1940s. He wore high-heeled
Hyer boots, custom made in Olathe, Kansas, and he rode
broncs at rodeos and celebrations all over northwestern Kansas
and eastern Colorado. This after a teenage bout with polio that
weakened one arm. "The doctor said to me, 'You can't ride
horses,' and I told him, 'The hell I can't.'" Nealis still spoke with
defiance some three-quarters of a century later.

His wife recalled his last bronc ride, when some of the
locals tried to trick him. The horse, supposedly an easy
bucker that ordinarily was used by kids to bring in milk cows,
didn't buck when he got on, so Nealis fanned him with his
hat and sank his spurs into his shoulders. Then, his wife
laughed, he got all the ride he wanted, one that lasted for
over five minutes and left him with no buttons on his shirt.
"But he rode him," she said.

"For years and years the only way to travel was on a saddle
horse," Nealis said. "Then I got a broken foot and when I got
older I had to quit riding. I'd like to set on a horse again, if
they would lift me on." His wife responded, "Well, Harry is
going to put you on his horse one of these days and put you
out in the middle of a bunch of cattle and take your picture

and tell how you rounded them up." Whether or not he got
to take that final ride in Wallace County I don't know, but if
there's a place in the hereafter for old cowboys (even ones
who cuss) then Mike Nealis is surely horseback now.

15. *Jesse James, Grandpa Russell,*
Uncle Frank, and the Daltons

IS THERE a family with pioneer roots in the plains states that
doesn't have an outlaw story or two? Here are a couple from
both sides of our family.

I learned one of these tales while fishing with my wife's
maternal grandfather, the late Clyde Russell (who was reared
on Big Creek east of Chanute, Kansas, on a farm whose
patent had been signed by President Grant). It seems that
a stranger came by one evening (this was before Grandpa
Russell's birth) riding a spirited, beautiful black stallion. He
asked for supper, a stall for his horse, and permission to sleep
in the barn. All was granted, except that the stranger was
denied the barn; the family insisted that he sleep in the
house—and that he eat breakfast with them as well.

Next morning as they were finishing breakfast, a group of
men rode up and the stranger met them at the door, talked
softly with their leader, then went to saddle his horse. As the
men were galloping out of the farmyard, the family heard one
of the band call out, "Let's go, Jess," just as their late guest
turned in his saddle on his rearing horse to wave good-bye.
Under his plate at the breakfast table was a twenty-dollar gold
piece, tribute to the legendary generosity of Jesse James. I have
heard other stories of Jesse (sometimes disguised as a woman)
staying the night with a family and returning the favor by
presenting the poor but worthy housewife with a fifty-pound
sack of flour to bolster her meager larder. And often a gold
double eagle would be found at the bottom of the sack.

One of the outlaw stories from my side of the family is
about Uncle Frank Goodnight, who got his finger shot off by

the Dalton Gang. I don't remember Uncle Frank (who died when I was only a couple of years old), but I heard plenty about him from my father and uncle, who had been mightily impressed in their youth by his big-time cattle operation near Englewood, Kansas. Still, even though Dad knew that Uncle Frank had a finger missing, I had never heard this particular story until it was told me about his grandfather by Don Goodnight of Meade.

Uncle Frank spent his youth near Dexter, Kansas, in the southern Flint Hills. While in his late teens he and another boy made money one fall by custom-shelling corn. Good money. In fact, one autumn Saturday when some of their customers met the boys in town to settle up, Uncle Frank had over eight hundred dollars in his pockets. His partner told him that he'd better get the money in a safe place because Grat Dalton had been seen on the streets of Dexter earlier that day. So Uncle Frank put the money in the bank (which wouldn't seem to me to have been the safest place, considering the attitude of the Daltons toward banks, but it turned out that Uncle Frank knew what he was doing), then later that evening got into his wagon and started the drive to the family ranch.

The trail home led through a grove of trees in an unpopulated area, and in the darkness of the grove a voice rang out, ordering him to stop and give over the money—or whatever it is that outlaws yell. For some reason (bravery, or perhaps dread because he had no money to give over) the boy slapped the reins and the horses took off at a run, shots and yells ringing out. The outlaws soon quit the chase, but Uncle Frank kept running the horses—until one of them fell dead in the traces as they neared the house, victim of a gunshot wound. Once inside, Uncle Frank discovered that the middle finger of his left hand was hanging by a shred. He hadn't felt any pain from the bullet because of all the excitement, but he did feel it when the doctor amputated what was left.

I'm told that Uncle Frank usually wore buckskin gloves, and that the empty little finger of the left glove always stuck out, a reminder for the rest of his life of his close call with the notorious Dalton Gang.

Part Three

COWGIRLS

16. *The First Cowgirl*

TRADITION has it that Lucille Mulhall was the first woman ever to be called a cowgirl. She won that honorific from "that cowboy in the White House" after proving herself the best hand present on a prairie wolf hunt that had been organized to entertain old Rough Riding Teddy. There is no doubt that Mulhall could out-ride, out-rope, and out-jockey most of the cowboys of her day, and she might have been the first to bear the title, but there had been plenty of cowgirls before her. The women bronc riders of Buffalo Bill's Wild West Show, for instance, had been thrilling audiences since 1886. Not to mention all the ranch wives and farm girls who had worked with cattle from the time the plains were first settled.

Today the cowgirl is as much a part of the culture of the American West as is the cowboy, from rodeos to ranches to popular culture. Historically, however, cowgirls developed about a generation after the first cowboys of the late 1860s and early 1870s. As these young men (many, if not most, of whom were in their late teens or early twenties) returned home, or moved from Texas to other parts of the plains, they took up farming or ranching, married, and had families. As their children listened to the exciting stories of their fathers, many of this new generation also wanted to be cowhands. Easy enough for the boys to accomplish, back in the 1880s, but not so easy for the girls. One Kansas girl, however, did work as a drover on a cattle drive in 1888. From what I can tell, she was the first and the only woman on record to have done this kind of work in the old open-range, trail-driving days.

I don't know whether Willie Matthews, from Caldwell down in Sumner County, was her real name or not, but that's what she called herself when she hired on with Samuel Dunn Houston at Clayton, New Mexico, in the summer of 1888. She had to disguise herself as a boy in order to get the job, but once she was hired, the 19-year-old did her work well.

Ranch women helping brand cattle on the J. W. Lough Ranch in Scott County, Kansas, 1906. (Photo courtesy of Kansas State Historical Society.)

Houston was a trail boss for the Holt Cattle Company from 1886 through 1893, and on this particular drive, from New Mexico to the Montana line, he was having all sorts of problems: alkali water, dry drives, trouble-making cowhands. But the new hand was a dandy: "I put him with the horses and put my rustler with the cattle. . . . The kid would get up the darkest stormy nights and stay with the cattle until the storm was over. He was good natured, very modest, didn't use any cuss words or tobacco, and was always pleasant. . . . I was so pleased with him that I wished many times that I could find two or three more like him."

After four months and several hundred miles on the trail, the herd crossed the Kansas Pacific Railroad near the Wyoming line. At that point Matthews got homesick to return to Caldwell, so "he" drew "his" time from Houston and headed out. A little while later the cowboys watched in amazement as a young woman in a dress and sunbonnet appeared out of nowhere and walked across the prairie toward them. As she drew within a few feet of the campfire, an astounded Houston said, "Kid, is it possible that you are a lady?"

Matthews was indeed a girl, and this is the story she told Houston and her fellow trailhands:

My papa is an old-time trail driver from Southern Texas. He drove from Texas to Caldwell, Kansas, in the '70s. He liked the country around Caldwell very much, so the last trip he made he went to work on a ranch up there and never returned to Texas any more. . . . I used to hear papa talk so much about the old cow trail and I made up my mind that . . . I was going up the trail if I had to run off. I had a pony of my own and read in the paper of the big herds passing Clayton, so I said, now is my chance. . . . I saddled my pony and told brother I was going out in the country, and I might be gone for a week, but for him to tell papa not to worry about me, I would be back. I had on a suit of brother's clothes and a pair of his boots. In three or four days I was in Clayton looking for a job and I found one. . . . Mr. Houston, I am glad I found you to make the trip with, for I have enjoyed it. I am going just as straight home as I can and that old train can't run too fast for me, when I get on it.

Houston and the rest of the hands thought so highly of the girl that they all, except for one man left to guard the herd, accompanied her to the depot and put her on the train. And then Houston hired *three* men to take her place on the drive.

I don't know if Willie Matthews was the only trail-driving cowgirl, but she is the only one recorded in Marvin Hunter's massive (over a thousand pages) collection of old-timers' memoirs, *The Trail Drivers of Texas*. So until another candidate comes along, this adventuresome teenager from the old cow town of Caldwell deserves the honor of being recognized as the world's first cowgirl.

I only wish that I knew her real name. And what she told her parents when she got home. Was her trail-driving father proud of her accomplishment, or did he punish her for running away in the first place? Did she marry and have children? Are any of her grandchildren around today? I'd sure like to hear the stories she told them about her experiences on the cow trail.

17.   *Kansas and the Cowgirl*

THE ORIGINS of the Great American Cowboy in all his manifestations—folk hero, movie star, rodeo performer, ranch hand—can be traced to the cattle drives after the Civil War, but those of the American cowgirl, are not so clearly discerned. During the quarter-century heyday of the big trail drives, women seem to have played a very small role in the physical work of the cattle business, at least on the big ranches. Roundup crews in Texas were all male, including the cooks, and while some ranch women might have helped gather and sort cattle, no one bothered to record their stories.

As with the cowboy, Kansas played an important role in the development of the cowgirl. In fact, as far as I am aware and as described in the previous chapter, the only girl ever to have come up the trail as a drover in the old days was a Kansan. Working cowgirls, from what I can surmise, originated during the final decades of the nineteenth century in much the same way as Willie Matthews had: as the trail-driving era came to an end, children of the old-time drovers were maturing and becoming involved in cattle work. Most of this new generation of cowhands was male, but there were some cowgirls among them, probably the most famous and certainly the best of whom was Lucille Mulhall. Mulhall came from the Cherokee Strip country of Oklahoma and was acknowledged to be the equal (many thought the superior) of any man alive in skill with a lariat rope and ability to ride a bucking horse. According to local tradition in the Flint Hills, the Mulhalls at one time pastured some cattle along the Verdigris River between Matfield Green and Madison. I am told by old-time Flint Hills ranchers that young cowhands in the area were infatuated with Lucille, as much by her horsemanship and cattle-working skills as by her good looks. Young Arthur Crocker, who had met the Mulhalls while he was herding cattle near Camp Creek, bought a fast horse from Lucille and ran it in local races near Matfield Green and Bazaar.

Although women such as Mulhall were beginning to take a more active part in ranch work by the turn of the century, as suggested by a 1906 photograph from the Lough Ranch in Scott County showing women roping and branding, probably the biggest influence in the development of the cowgirl was the Wild West show. Sharpshooter Annie Oakley, a star of Buffalo Bill's show, was among the first and certainly the most famous of these early performers, but many others were soon to be found riding alongside the cowboys in romanticized displays of the taming of the frontier.

Some cowgirls, such as Jackie Laird of Ponca City, Oklahoma (see chapter 19) rode for big-time shows. Other Wild West show cowgirls were less famous and operated on a much smaller scale, as did, for instance, Mrs. Curley Griffit (I haven't been able to learn her first name), one member of a three-person Wild West troupe that performed at the 1923 Burdick Field Day fair and rodeo. All three trick rode and fancy roped. For a special exhibition Curley and another cowboy bulldogged steers and Mrs. Griffit rode bucking broncs.

In addition to Wild West exhibitions, cowgirls competed in early-day rodeos throughout Kansas and the Great Plains. Most rodeos during the first three or four decades of this century featured a number of events for women—relay races, trick roping, trick riding, cow (or steer) riding, bulldogging, and saddle bronc riding. Women, as did men at this time, usually rode steers with a two-handed surcingle. In the bronc-riding event, however, women were allowed to tie their stirrups down, which gives the rider an advantage in staying aboard a bucking horse.

Goldie Offutt of Garden City, whose husband Dan was one of the top rodeo cowboys in the nation, was an excellent cow and steer rider. Many photographs of cowgirls riding broncs and steers at Kansas rodeos have survived, as has one showing Grace Runyon bulldogging a steer from the running board of an automobile at the 1929 Kiowa rodeo. The most remark-able cowgirl photograph I have seen, however, is one show-ing Mattie Downs riding a bucking horse at a 1935 rodeo in either Chase or Greenwood county. The ride itself is not that remarkable, but the cowgirl is; according to my informant, Downs was delivered of a baby only seventeen days after the bronc ride—a full-term, normal, healthy baby. I don't know much else about her except that after she rode to the whistle she refused to dismount until the pickup man had brought the bronc to a complete standstill—she said she didn't want to get hurt!

Some rodeo events, such as trick riding, were open to both men and women contestants, but contests were usually segregated. Rarely were women allowed to enter men's events, although when women such as Prairie Rose Hender-son or Lucille Mulhall did get a chance to enter an open event they often won, as did one Kansas cowgirl in calf-roping contests in the north central Flint Hills of the 1930s. Helen Ebbetts Olson, daughter of locally renowned cowman Bill Ebbetts, was, I am told, one of the best ropers in the area and regularly beat the cowboys in the local rodeos.

Sometime around the beginning of World War II rodeos quit having women's bronc and steer riding events and at roughly the same time they completed the conversion of both men's and women's trick roping and trick riding from contests to exhibitions. Well before this time, however, Malee Harding of Coldwater had earned a national reputation as a trick rider and roper. Harding's older sister preceded her in the rodeo arena, performing at area rodeos when she was still a schoolgirl, as recorded in the *Coldwater Talisman* of October 14, 1926: "Darlene Harding, Coldwater's own cowgirl . . . handles a rope with the best of them. Her rope spinning was good and she proved herself adept at the art. Her younger sister who showed that she, too, could handle a rope, claimed some of the honors with Miss Darlene."

Malee Harding was only six years old at the time. Within five years she had indeed claimed her share of the honors, according to information supplied to me by Evelyn Reed, librarian at Coldwater. Harding had performed with the Hagenbeck-Wallace Circus Wild West Show at eight years of age, and the following year (1929) she appeared at major rodeos throughout the United States and Canada. In 1930 she was the featured trick rider and fancy roper at the Calgary Stampede, whose organizers had this to say about her: "Malee Harding is undoubtedly one of the best performers we have ever had at our show." She even had her picture taken with President Coolidge. In addition to her rodeo work Harding was a drum major for the high school band, leading marches with a twirling rope instead of a baton. If the spectators at parades crowded in, she would enlarge the loop to hold them back.

Kansas has had many other trick riders over the years. One of the most successful during the 1950s was Melba Winey Prewitt of Butler County, who had a riding, roping, and trained-horse act that she took to professional rodeos throughout the country, some of which were produced by the Roberts Rodeo Company of Strong City. The Roberts family is unquestionably the most famous rodeo family in Kansas. E. C., the father, produced rodeos for many years and was named Rodeo Man of the Year in 1979. Ken, the oldest son, was world-champion bull rider from 1943 through 1945, while his younger brother Gerald was world all-around champion in 1942 and 1948.

Marge, the oldest child in the family, however, was the first to follow the rodeo circuit (see chapter 18). As a teenager she rode in the summertime for the Clyde Miller Wild West Show, based in Iowa, coming home each winter to attend high school. She rode steers and bucking horses and developed a trick-riding act that took her all over the country. One of her innovations in trick riding was the dive, in which she leaned rigidly far out over a running horse's neck at an almost impossible angle. In 1940 she won the women's bronc riding at Cheyenne, a feat that can fairly be compared to a world championship. Thus Marge Roberts can legitimately be said to have led the way into the world of rodeo for her two famous brothers. Her contributions to rodeo and to the heritage of the West were recognized in 1987 by her posthumous induction into the National Cowgirl Hall of Fame, located in Fort Worth, Texas.

Today hundreds of cowgirls are following in the footsteps of Marge Roberts, Malee Harding, Grace Runyon, Goldie Offutt, and many other pioneer Kansas cowgirls. Barrel racing may have replaced women's bronc riding at rodeos, but today's cowgirls can be found not only running barrels, but also heading and heeling at team ropings, riding in cutting-horse contests, competing in team penning contests, and working as trainers and jockeys at race tracks, among many other pursuits traditionally thought of as the prerogative of cowboys.

These competitive sports, however, show only one side of the cowgirl. More important in her maturation as an active partner in carrying on the traditions of cattle country is that cowgirls today no longer have to disguise themselves as boys in order to break horses and work cattle. In fact, I can readily think of at least three Flint Hills ranches within thirty miles of my home that are run by women. Rosalie Clymer of Council Grove not only raises livestock but shoes horses as well. Bobbie Hammond maintains the family tradition of caring for pasture cattle on the Nation Ranch in Chase County (on

Marge Roberts performing the dive, late 1940s. (Author's collection.)

Camp Creek near where Lucille Mulhall is said to have
looked after cattle nearly a century past). Jane Koger of Bazaar uses crews made up entirely of cowgirls to work and ship
cattle pastured on her extensive Chase County holdings.

Obviously the cowgirl tradition is alive and well in Kansas.
Willie Matthews really started something when she ran away
from home to join a trail crew a little over a hundred years
ago.

18.   *Marge Roberts, Hall of Fame Cowgirl*

LINDERMAN, Cooper, Tescher, Greenough, Ferguson, Combs—
throughout the years there have been a number of notable
rodeo families, many of them counting multiple world champions among their members. It is unlikely, however, that any
single family covered the spectrum of rodeo more fully than
did the Riding Robertses of Strong City, Kansas. Father E. C.
was a stock contractor, producer, and top-notch pickup man;
Ken was a three-time bull-riding world champion who later
joined his father in providing stock and producing rodeos;
Gerald was twice an all-around world champion who, after
retiring from the arena, has turned to manufacturing rodeo
equipment; and daughter Marge was a bronc rider and innovative trick rider who performed throughout the country.

It is Marge's career, in fact, that distinguishes the Robertses from many of the other famous rodeo families. There
have been several sets of brothers who have been world
champions, but I cannot recall any other brother-sister combination that could boast this achievement. Technically, I
suppose, Marge was not a world champion in that there was
no official world title in women's bronc riding when she won
Cheyenne in 1940. On the other hand, among rodeo folk in
the days before official world titles were instituted, winning
Cheyenne was tantamount to a championship, about as high
as one could go toward earning the respect of one's peers.

Thus in essence, if not in fact, Marge Roberts was the first in her celebrated family to become a Champion of the World.

In later years, after Marge had retired to stock raising in the Flint Hills just east of Strong City and was filling her leisure moments with oil painting, she rarely spoke of her earlier exploits in the rodeo arena, and then only modestly. Area residents who had seen her trick ride at the annual Flint Hills Rodeo, and who were well aware of the fame of her brothers, would assume that, and sometimes ask if, she had followed Ken and Gerald into rodeo. "No," was her quiet response, "they followed me." They had indeed followed her, not only in winning their world titles and, before that, into rodeo competition, but even into the world itself. Marjorie Mae Roberts (born July 3, 1916) was the eldest of the six children that would be born to Emmett and Mae Roberts who, at the time, lived in the Chalk community near Council Grove. Ken was born a couple of years later, and Gerald two years after that in October 1920 (or perhaps the spacing was a year and a half between births; Gerald says he was born in 1919 and that the confusion arises from having had to lie so much about his age when he was first starting to rodeo so that neither he nor his parents could ever recall his birthdate with certainty). Howard and Clifford were also born in Morris County, with Gloria coming along after the family had moved southwest fifteen miles to a farm near Strong City in 1931. Marge was fourteen at the time and had already begun to rodeo.

She had started riding horses at the tender age of six months when her father would set her on the back of his saddle horse while he unharnessed his work team, fed the cattle, milked the cows, and finished his evening chores. The Roberts place was always full of horses. E. C. earned extra money as the neighborhood horse breaker and would occasionally buy wild horses a carload at a time to break and sell, but he never let any of his children ride a pony; he always mounted them on full-sized horses. The children rode to school, honing skills that would later take them to the top. Everett Brammell, principal of Strong City High School dur-

ing the early 1930s, recalls seeing the three eldest Roberts
children loping across the hills "looking like they were born
on a horse." Even in grade school Marge would, once out of
sight of her father, run her horse across the prairies all the
way to school. "The horse had all day to rest," she would say
in recounting the memory. Sometimes she would go at a
slower lope, but standing up on the saddle, developing a
sense of balance that would later make her a top trick rider.

Marge and Ken and Gerald all joined in helping their
father break horses. E. C. would sell off the gentled colts and
replace them with wild ones just as quickly as the kids would
get them trained. (A side note: despite his excellent reputation as a bronc rider, the elder Roberts never competed in
rodeos. I find it interesting, however, that whenever a horse
one of the kids was breaking proved hard to ride, Emmett
would get aboard and take the buck out of him.) After moving to Chase County Marge and Ken would often go back to
the Council Grove area to pick up some colts from former
neighbors. "By the time they rode them home fifteen or
twenty miles," E. C. recalls, "they had them pretty well broke
already." The kids had rigged up a chute in the barn lot,
where they not only saddled the colts to be broken but also
rode the work horses and mules, the milk cows, and the stock
cows and bulls—anything on the place that might buck. Gerald recalls that, before Marge started rodeoing she rode a
bronc just like a man did, without tying down the stirrups.
"When she was learning, she rode just like Ken and I did.
We'd put rodeos on at home on Sunday afternoons and
neighbors would come in and sometimes pass the hat for us.
We'd get five or six dollars. I rode every cow and every bull
on the place. We all three just took turns riding them." These
impromptu Sunday afternoon buckouts, which began in the
early 1930s, evolved into the Flint Hills Rodeo, which held its
fifty-seventh annual performance in 1994.

Just when Marge began riding professionally is not clear,
but family members recall that she was riding steers at some
of the nearby small amateur and pasture rodeos during her
first year in high school when she was only thirteen years old.

Don Bell of Byron, Wyoming, recalls 1931 as the first time he ever saw her ride. The occasion was a Rufus Rollins bronc show in Kansas City's Swope Park. Rollins, who worked in the Kansas City stockyards (and who had earlier served time as part of the Henry Starr outlaw gang), had some broncs and some canvas side walls he would set up wherever he thought there were enough people gathered to pass a hat after the riding was over. On this particular occasion, Marge had approached Rollins and told him that she'd like to ride. He responded that he "didn't have any girls' broncs, only tough horses." She said that she wanted a bad one, so Rollins cut out one of his worst and cinched on a two-handed bareback rigging (standard for both men and women at the time). Bell loaned her his boots and spurs, and she made a fine ride (despite the loss of one of the over-large boots) and collected her three dollars' mount money. Crowds loved to watch Marge ride, Bell told me, because she was showy and always seemed to be having a lot of fun. She would whoop and holler throughout the ride, and invariably had a big grin on her face, creating a spectacle unmatched by any of the other women bronc riders Bell knew.

During the summer of her sixteenth year Marge learned that the Clyde Miller Wild West Show would be in Sidney, Iowa, so she hitchhiked there and hired on at ten dollars a week, riding in some of the routines and doing simple trick riding. Mrs. Miller, upon learning the girl's age, insisted on driving her back to Strong City, where an agreement was reached that Marge could continue with the troupe in the summer so long as she returned home in the fall in time for her high school classes. The next summer, 1933, was her first full season as a performing cowgirl. Ken accompanied her as a member of the Miller show that year, while Gerald, just out of the eighth grade, hitchhiked to Nebraska to join his brother as a steer rider. He was sent back home after a couple of weeks when he was thrown off, knocked unconscious for several hours, and the Millers found out that he was only thirteen.

Marge continued with the Miller Wild West Show for four

years, acquiring not only riding experience but a husband as well. In 1934, the same year she was graduated from high school, Marge married Eddie Boysen of Sioux Falls, South Dakota, a bronc rider, bulldogger, and trick roper. The entire Miller troupe attended the wedding. In 1937 the Boysens left Clyde Miller and struck out on the rodeo circuit, both competing and contracting their specialty acts. They also promoted some smaller rodeos. About this time Marge also did some trick riding for the Barnes Circus and the Cole Brothers Circus.

Winning the women's bronc riding at Cheyenne in 1940 may have been Marge's highest personal achievement in rodeo, but her longest-lasting influence was undoubtedly in trick riding, where she not only perfected such classic routines as the head stand and "death drag," but also invented the dive, in which she stood at the withers of a running horse and leaned stiffly ahead at a forty-five degree angle, her hands extending well beyond the horse's ears. Serendipity, as usual, played its innovating role in the development of this stunt, which had its origins in a standard saddle stand at one of the Miller shows. Marge, riding Buck, her favorite mount, lost her balance and started leaning forward, ending out far over Buck's neck. His speed and the wind resistance kept her from falling, and the crowd's enthusiastic response let Marge know that this was an act to develop. Gerald Roberts recalls that many other female trick riders took up the "dive" after Marge had invented it, but they were never as good. "Marge would lean out there at kind of an angle, just like that, right over that horse's head," he told me, demonstrating with his hands together high over his head, "That horse he run so fast he would let her do that. His gait was just right to hold her up, like a plane taking off when the wind hits the wings just right. After that horse died, she never could get another horse that could do the trick so good."

Buck died, by the way, from eating on a bale of bad hay, made from a kind of grass that punctures the intestines, en route to Colorado to perform at a rodeo. Marge returned to Oklahoma for a spotted mare she also used in her act, not thinking to change the hay in the manger of the horse trailer. The mare ate it and died as well. Marge quit trick riding a few years later, never again finding a horse that could perform stunts as well or carry her as successfully as had Buck. One of the last rodeos in which she performed was her hometown show, the Flint Hills Rodeo, in 1952.

Sometime in the early 1940s (records aren't available and family members are unclear) Marge's marriage to Eddie Boysen broke up, and she married George "Kid" Roberts sometime shortly thereafter. Stories one hears indicate that Kid was something of a ladies' man and that the marriage was rocky throughout its five- or six-year run. Kid did some rodeoing, but he was also an aficionado of the track, and it was during this time that Marge acquired a string of race-horses. She and her second husband were successful on tracks ranging from Arizona, Oregon, and Washington to Illinois. Marge trained her own horses and even attempted a jockey's career, but that lasted only a few weeks. Her most successful horse was one she bred herself, Slim Pickins, named after the rodeo clown who later became a well-known movie actor.

During the 1940s Marge wintered in Tucson, where she sometimes worked on dude ranches, an experience she cap-italized on in 1952 when she acquired the horseback riding concession at Lake of the Ozarks State Park near Camden-ton, Missouri, a business she ran for some ten years. By this time her second marriage had broken up and she was back with, although not married to, Eddie Boysen, who lived with her in Camdenton and helped run the stable. E. C., who, as usual, was heavily involved in the horse business, located about thirty-five horses for Marge to buy and haul to Mis-souri. Tourist season began in late spring and ran through early fall, at which time Marge would load the horses onto one of the Roberts Rodeo semis and send them to Strong City to winter in the Flint Hills.

The contract with Missouri gave Marge sole riding rights in the state park, but a competing stable owner on adjoining private land infringed on her operation by cutting the fences so that he could lead tourists along the forest trails that were supposed to be the major attraction of the state franchise that Marge had paid for. Frequent complaints to the offender did no good, nor did appeals to local law enforcement officials, who did not seem overly eager to take steps against a "local" in a dispute with an out-of-stater. Fence repairs would last only until the competing stable owner's next trip into the forest. In 1957 he came upon Eddie Boysen and a fifteen-year-old hired boy as they were fixing fence. In the ensuing argument, both were shot and killed. An Ozark jury acquitted the man of Eddie's murder, but apparently the deliberate killing of a teenage witness was too much: he was convicted of that crime, but received only a ten-year sentence.

Marge continued to run the riding stable after Eddie's death. In 1959 she met Al Hart aboard the *Larry Don,* a dinner-dance cruise boat at Lake of the Ozarks. Al, a professional pilot, operated a sea-plane concession at the lake. They married two years later and bought land just east of Strong City. For the next two years they would winter in Kansas, then return to Missouri to run their concessions in the summer.

In 1963, however, they moved permanently to the Flint Hills. At that time there were several large feedlots in Chase County, and Marge would buy the unwanted baby calves dropped by heifers on feed, then hand feed them until they were large enough to resell for a profit. The better heifer calves she would keep, eventually building up a herd of some 170 cows. She also learned how to artificially inseminate and used this means to develop a good purebred string of Guernsey and Maine-Anjou cows. The Harts sold their herd in 1981 so that they would be more free to travel, especially to Tucson to visit old rodeo friends such as Alice and Marge Greenough and Betty Hazen. The Harts also wintered, in a travel trailer, in Mexico on the Pacific at San Carlos.

Al Hart told me a couple of revealing anecdotes about his wife, the first of which shows Marge's ability as a rodeo competitor: "I heard Marge say that she once got her brothers out of hock. They had gone to a little punkin roller rodeo, probably no farther away than Newton. They called her and said that they owed the hotel five dollars for a room and another five for food, and they weren't winning anything at the rodeo. So she hitchhiked there and won the women's steer riding, got them out of hock, and bought them a steak dinner. She said she even had a few dollars left when she got home. Her father never said a word to the boys, but he gave her the devil for running away and riding there." About all these admonitions from E. C. and Marge's mother did, however, was to ensure that she would graduate from high school. As E. C. told me, "She'd rather rodeo than go to school, but we never had much trouble with her. The boys, though, they finally quit."

Al also told of Marge riding in the Flint Hills Rodeo parade when she was in her sixties: "One of the local ranchers would ask if she'd like to ride, and she'd say, 'Sure.' Then they'd bring in some green broke horse for her, maybe he'd only been saddled once, or maybe just haltered. Some of the cowboys would hold it for her while she got on, but once she was in the saddle, she was on it. You could see her coming down the parade route sideways, the horse snorting and prancing. The riders in front and back of her always gave her plenty of room. When the parade would pass by the church in Strong City, her mother would always be sitting there, and she'd tell her, 'Marjorie, that horse is going to hurt you.' But no horse ever did."

Marge died of cancer on April 23, 1982. The progress of the disease was sudden after its initial diagnosis, Gerald Roberts told me. He was out of state at the time, and Marge was dead before he was able to drive back. Her multifaceted career as a cowgirl, circus performer, horsewoman, and cattle rancher had started in the Flint Hills of Kansas and had taken her throughout the country. She won Cheyenne, rode in Madison Square Garden, competed in the Powder Puff Horse Race in Boston, and rodeoed all over the country, including the states of Minnesota, Nebraska, Oregon, Texas, Washington, Missouri, Oklahoma, Colorado, Arizona, South Dakota, California, Utah, and Iowa, among others.

"Everything she did, she did on her own," Gerald Roberts told me. Fortunately, some of her friends in Chase County saw fit to collect and recount the contributions Marge Roberts made to rodeo and to western heritage. Her nomination to the National Cowgirl Hall of Fame was approved, and she was inducted in 1987, appropriately enough, the same year that the rodeo she helped to found, the Flint Hills Rodeo, celebrated its golden anniversary.

19.   *Jackie Laird, Rider for the 101*

BACK IN 1987 I had the privilege of meeting the last surviving cowgirl to have ridden for the famous Miller Brothers 101 Ranch Wild West Show. Mary Ellen Lease McFarlin Laird, named for the Kansas populist agitator and nicknamed Jackie, was born in 1896 in what had once been the Cherokee Strip. Her parents worked for the 101 Ranch, her father milking cows (seventy-five head by hand twice a day until 1903 or 1904, when the 101 bought the first automated milking machines in Oklahoma) and her mother cooking for the two hundred–plus full-time employees of the formidable ranch-farm-business-entertainment conglomerate that was the 101 Ranch.

Laird started earning money from the 101 when she was around ten, helping to gather eggs from the flock of two thousand white leghorn hens. She would start each day at sundown, after the heat had let up, and for two hours would gather eggs, putting them in a cart pushed by one of the farmhands. She and her younger sister also helped their father by riding after the milk cows, which shared a pasture with a large herd of somewhat unpredictable bison and even more unpredictable longhorns. She remembers seeing a pony walking a treadmill alongside the milk house, providing churning power for the fifty pounds of butter produced by the 101 each day.

Laird showed me a photograph of herself and "old Tony bear," a ranch pet she had helped raise when he was brought back as an orphan cub from a hunt in New Mexico. Tony loved to eat ice cream but preferred pop or near beer from the bottle, reaching out to grab hold of a pant leg until the drinker would give up his treat to the bear. Once when Tony had unintentionally been left untended for several days, Laird walked up to him and playfully said, "Do you know me?" Instead of playing back, as he usually did, the hungry bear suddenly reached out and ripped her arm from the elbow through the hand. The scar was still clearly visible. "I was just bleeding awful," she told me, "and they put me on an old gray mule and sent me to Ponca City and told me to find a doctor. I'd never been to Ponca in my life, but they said 'Just follow the road.' I can still see that old mule's ears afloppin'." She reached Ponca City, found a drugstore, figured there should be a doctor's office nearby, and found one upstairs. So she got her wound treated, then rode back home. Pretty brave for a twelve-year-old girl.

Laird trick rode for the 101 Wild West from 1914 to 1926. When England's George V visited the 101, Queen Mary complimented Laird on her pretty black hair and said, "You must come to see me sometime," which is one reason she was picked to accompany the show to England in 1914. While they were there, World War I broke out and the government confiscated all the horses and mules of the show for the war effort, sending the cowboys, cowgirls, and Indians back to America. Laird also accompanied the show to South America and Germany, in addition to performing all over the United States.

Because of her role in the Wild West show, Laird met many of the famous western heroes of the day, including Bill Pickett, the legendary African American cowboy (or the "dusky demon," as the posters of the time advertised him) who invented the sport of bulldogging—by biting a steer in the lip and pulling him to the ground with tooth-power only. She also knew Buffalo Bill Cody, who, in ill health and broke, spent the last couple of years of his life touring with the Miller Brothers show. Now there are lots of stories about Buffalo Bill, and lots of opinions about his bona fides as a western hero, but from what I've been able to figure out he was an unusual combination of the real McCoy and a show-business image. Charles Goodnight, for instance, was the real McCoy, whereas John Wayne (that Iowegian who couldn't sit a horse worth a damn) was straight show biz. But Buffalo Bill really did hunt buffalo for the Kansas Pacific Railroad, and he really was an Indian scout for the army. Then during the winter he'd go back to Chicago and play himself on stage, hunting buffalo and fighting Indians amid romanticized scenery. But during the summer, he'd go back out onto the plains and hunt buffalo and fight Indians.

Cody had the vision to realize that the West was changing, was closing up, so fairly early on (1882) he began putting together what would become his world famous Wild West show. Besides establishing the stereotype of the mythic West, this show also made Cody America's first show-business super-star, our first entertainment giant, our first popular media megahero. Think of it this way: if there had been super-markets with checkout-lane gantlets to run back in his heyday, Buffalo Bill's face would have appeared as regularly on the tabloid scandal sheets as Madonna's or Liz Taylor's or Michael Jackson's do today. More seriously, given the permeating influence that the cowboy myth has had on American life, it would be hard to overstate the cultural importance of Buffalo Bill.

Jackie Laird knew this man personally, had performed with him in the Wild West show, had seen and presumably talked with him in back of the arena or in the mess tent or on the train as they traveled between shows. She knew firsthand one of the icons of the American West. And here was my chance to touch, at only one remove, this cultural giant, this American legend.

"Tell me about Buffalo Bill," I said. "What was he like?"

And her reply, verbatim I will quote it: "He was a mean old son of a bitch. I didn't like him."

After pushing my jaw back up, I asked why and got this story. It seems that the show was performing in New York, an outdoor performance at night. Laird, a teenager at the time, was playing the role of a pioneer girl crossing the plains with her family in a covered wagon. The pageant called for them to be attacked by Indians, and then to be saved by Buffalo Bill leading a charge of cavalry. Because it was night, the Indians were carrying torches instead of spears, and because it was windy, one of the torches accidentally set the covered wagon afire. Jackie's costume caught fire as well, and she ran screaming from the wagon. When Buffalo Bill jumped off his horse to roll her in the dirt and put out the flames, he growled at her, "What are you doing? Trying to crowd the act? Now dammit, get over there where you belong!"

Whether his comment was genuinely surly or, more likely, an expression of worried nervousness, what Laird remembered three-quarters of a century later, as clearly as she remembered the audience, not recognizing the fire as an accident, on its feet cheering for an encore as she was being carried off to the hospital, was a grumpy old man who accused her of hogging the show.

Laird was ninety-one when I visited with her at the Pioneer Woman Museum in Ponca City in 1987. When Jan Prough and Laura Streich brought her down to the museum, Laird was in her wheelchair, a felt cowboy hat sitting comfortably on her head. I interviewed her in the entry hall of the museum, where she sat directly underneath an oil painting of herself as a young trick rider with the 101 Wild West Show. The painting showed a handsome girl in her twenties, wearing a green velvet riding costume, elbow-length fringed buckskin gloves, and a ten-gallon Stetson from under which spilled long black hair. As the occasional visitor would enter the museum, Prough or Streich would quietly point to Laird and to the painting. And Laird, over sixty years since she had been that girl who performed before cheering crowds, would straighten and smile her show smile. For just a moment her hair was once again long and black, her polyester pants green velvet riding breeches, and her wheelchair a rearing horse.

Postscript
Jackie Laird died on December 4, 1990. She was ninety-four years old.

20. *Women Jockeys*

I REMEMBER a big stir a decade or so back when women jockeys suddenly burst onto the scene. One of them got her picture on the cover of *Sports Illustrated* and another married Fred Astaire—or maybe it was the same one. Whatever the case, the media fell over itself detailing how the male chauvinist paddock (and winner's circle) had finally been sexually integrated.

I hate to disillusion the editors at *Sports Illustrated,* but women jockeys, at least in Kansas, are nothing new and haven't been for at least half a century. I remember as a boy going to the dirt track near Conway Springs with Grandpa Rice (this was just after World War II) to watch the races, many of which were won by a local girl, Joyce Riggs. She was picking up quite a bit of regional fame about that time. I was rummaging around in an antique store sometime back and found a copy of the *Wichita Beacon* for June 1, 1946. There on the sports page was a local racing item ("Girl Jockey Rides Horse to Victory") and two photographs of Riggs, an action shot of the finish and a close-up at the weigh-in. Another girl, Betty Joe Bryant, was also riding in the five-day meet (held at Yochum Track on South Seneca).

I don't know how long Joyce Riggs pursued her racing career, but not long ago I talked to a woman who has jockeyed all over the central and southern plains for some quarter of a century. Marjorie Jean Arford (née Frui) rode in her first race shortly after she married her husband John in 1930—she was nineteen, he twenty-one. I stopped to visit the Arfords early in May 1985 on the farm between Norton and Almena where Marjorie's parents had lived and where they themselves have spent all their adult lives—that is, when they haven't been on the road with racehorses.

Marjorie is a small, wiry, animated woman who loves animals. There were twin bottle-fed calves looking up from the barn lot, excited dogs giving me a good sniffing over, cats both running and sunning, and a young appaloosa in the corral (Marjorie's latest acquisition—she can't quit riding).

She invited me and her daughter-in-law (Ada, wife of John, Jr.) into the kitchen (the country kitchen that we all remember from visiting our great-aunt or our grandmother when we were little—painted wooden cabinets, linoleum-covered floor, a permeation of coffee) and gave me a piece of freshly baked mulberry pie. Then she and John began to tell me what racing was like back in the 1930s.

It was actually pretty good—better than straight farming, if you had fast horses. John said that he never had a net annual loss until after he quit racing in the mid-1950s. Once, he said, he bought a combine, paying half down, then went to Cheyenne for the Frontier Days (which has always had a big racing card in addition to the rodeo), where Marjorie rode in both regular and girls' races. They ran into the implement dealer there, who was more than a little surprised when John handed over the rest of the combine payment, money made on the track by his horses.

Back in those days most of the county seat towns in Kansas, and many other towns besides, had dirt tracks—bush tracks, the pari-mutuel, people call them—where anyone with a fast horse could try his luck. The races tended to be a little longer than modern quarter-horse races, not quite so long as those at regular thoroughbred tracks. Most of the horses the Arfords owned were not registered but had a goodly strain of thoroughbred running through their veins.

Their two best horses were Sleepy John (originally leased, then bought, from a neighboring farmer) and Moreanon (a big-ankled black horse from Santa Anita that John nursed back to racing form) and their best year was 1939. That year the Arfords raced, among other places, in Norton, Stockton, Liberal, Phillipsburg, and Smith Center, Kansas; North Platte, Beaver City, Burwell, and Broken Bow, Nebraska; Cheyenne, Wyoming; Tulsa and Alva, Oklahoma; and Albuquerque, New Mexico. Marjorie rode Sleepy John and Moreanon to seventeen victories each that season.

I asked about injuries. When Marjorie said that she had never broken any bones riding, both John and Ada snorted; apparently they took her injuries more seriously than she

did. She did get a fracture at Norton in 1940, but not actually
in the race. They were using some cobbled-up wooden starting gates, she told me, and "this silly old horse wouldn't go
in," so she was behind him hitting him with a switch, "and
the danged old thing kicked me and broke my arm."

Her worst track mishap was at Brush, Colorado, when she
was riding Moreanon. A couple of horses went down, one
right in front of her, and Moreanon flip-flopped, sending
her flying over his head so fast that she stripped the bridle
and blinders off as she went. Her mount scrambled to his feet
and finished the race while she sat there amid the wreckage.
Two horses had to be destroyed, but Marjorie was unshaken;
she rode the next day.

Life on the road was exciting, but not easy. The Arfords,
living in wheat country, could plant in the fall, harvest in
early summer, and have the rest of the year for horses. A
hundred dollars back then was more than enough money to
get them to, through, and back from the entire Frontier Days
at Cheyenne, what with cheap gasoline, pork and beans, and
potted-meat sandwiches. They had money enough to eat better, Marjorie said, but she just didn't have time to cook, look
after a baby, and ride horses too. Johnny, Jr., was born in the
summer of 1938; Marjorie was racing a month later.

John Arford affects indifference about his feelings toward
horses, but he is especially proud of having been able to take
a horse that others had given up on and turn it into a winner.
Moreanon, for instance, he picked up, big ankles and all,
from a couple of Coloradans who had bought him in San
Antonio after he was shipped back from California.

Sleepy John required more than careful nursing. He would
run great for three-eighths of a mile, then just seem to quit.
John, after some close observation, finally figured out that
the horse was swallowing his tongue and choking at about
that distance, so he took a dish towel, looped the middle
around the horse's tongue, and tied the ends under his chin
so he couldn't swallow it. From then on Sleepy John could
run and win the longer races.

One of Marjorie's favorite mounts was Mary Heathen (I

wonder if the original owners didn't mean "Merry"?), a mare
that she rode to many wins over the years, including her last
race in 1952. Marjorie's racing career spanned nearly a quarter of a century and took her over half a dozen states. She
doesn't recall just how many races she has run or won, but
she did say that she had to earn every victory. Chivalry
stopped at the starting gates; down the straightaway it was
every jockey for him (and her) self.

Today women jockeys are fairly commonplace. In fact,
one of our former neighbors, Tammy Wessel, now trains running quarter horses in Texas and does some jockeying as well.
Wessel won her first race the summer of 1985 at Eureka
Downs in Greenwood County, but she (and others like her)
probably wouldn't even be in the business if it weren't for the
pioneering of women like Marjorie Arford.

21. *Dorothy Branson and the Old Mule Barn*

A WHILE back I was visiting with Dorothy Branson of Manhattan, Kansas, who told me about a huge mule barn on a ranch
near Medicine Lodge where she spent her youth. Old barns,
particularly unusual ones or those with a distinctive history,
really whet my interest, so I asked her to send me some
information about it. Her letter described not only the barn
but rural life of the 1920s.

The barn itself, with three cupolas (home for pigeons and
sparrows) and two haymows (where Branson played with kit-
tens), was large enough to hold a hundred mules, but Branson doesn't know who built it. It was there when her grandfather and father, Al and John Hybsha, bought the sixteen
hundred acre ranch in 1919. For those who haven't been
there, Medicine Lodge is in the Gypsum Hills, some of the
roughest, prettiest landscape in all the plains. The big pasture on their ranch, where her father's Herefords grazed, had
tree-filled canyons, buffalo wallows, and a prairie-dog town.

There was also a little pasture for the milk cows. Branson

started milking at age eight. Her father would milk the four hardest cows, and she the four easiest. One of her jobs was to bring the milk cows in on Jimmy, her cow pony. She also helped with the branding when she got older. Feeding chickens, gathering eggs, and tending one of the two family gardens were her regular chores. They raised beets, beans, carrots, strawberries, cantaloupes, tomatoes, potatoes (sweet and Irish), peanuts, and popcorn. Watermelons were so plentiful that first one neighbor then another would have watermelon parties throughout the summer.

During harvest time and hay season, Branson and her sister helped their mother and grandmother feed the big work crews. Her grandfather would bring hot water from the house and chop the heads off four chickens, then the girls would scald, pluck, and clean them. Winter was hog-butchering time, and Branson remembers helping to render lard and make sausage, a special Czech variety called *esirnetze*. They would clean the intestines for casing, then stuff the ground meat in with a piece of cattle horn. "I have never eaten better sausage, but I could not handle all the pork—I would be sick every night. But I lived!"

Life on the ranch was not all work, however. There was a cabin at each of the two ponds in the big cattle pasture, and the girls and their friends would ride, fish, boat, picnic, and have slumber parties there. In winter they would take little red sleds, made by their grandfather, to North Antelope school. There they would play fox and geese with the Chapin, Weidner, and Watkins kids. In warmer weather they played ball, built a dugout, and "marched endlessly to the tune of 'A belly full of beans and you can't keep step.'" Usually they walked the two and a half miles to school, but sometimes they rode their ponies and had horse races on the dirt road. Automobile traffic was "no more than one car a week."

Sometime around 1940 her father sold out to the Chain Ranch, which is still one of the big ranching operations near Medicine Lodge. About twenty years ago Branson went back for a visit and found a beautiful stone house instead of the two frame houses used by the Hybshas. The old red barn had been covered with tin and the cupolas and mangers and stalls removed. The barn was filled with hay, not mules, and "the parklike place where the pitcher pump and our swings and playhouse had been was all tall brush and weeds." Life has a way of doing that with childhood, too, doesn't it?

Part Four

ANIMALS

ONE NICE summer afternoon in 1989 Cathy and I took a drive down into the Flint Hills. We had a picnic at Camp Creek (where Zebulon Pike is reputed to have crossed the Verdigris and given the Hills their name in 1806), then drove up to the cattle pens on the Kansas Turnpike and took the cattle trail across to Sharpes Creek. We must have gone through ten miles or so of nothing but cattle, tallgrass, wildflowers, and wildlife, including two jackrabbits (an unusual sight these days) and a badger.

Badgers are not an endangered species in the Flint Hills, but you don't see one out in the daylight all that often either. This happened to be the first one I had seen in the wild for some time, but by chance one had visited our house just a couple of days earlier. Actually he was in the garage. As I drove in about midnight, I saw two of the dogs in the head-lights, barking at what I thought at first was an opossum (they sometimes come in to raid the dog food), then a raccoon. But when I heard the growling and hissing I knew it was no possum or coon.

For those who think badgers are nice creatures, like the ones children read about in *The Wind in the Willows* or the books about Frances the badger, let me assure you that they are fierce. This wasn't the biggest badger I had ever seen, but it was full grown with bearlike claws that can dig faster than a tractor-powered post-hole auger, and I have never before heard hissing as loud as that coming out of the corner where he huddled under a ladder away from the dogs.

Not that our dogs are ever in imminent danger of being bitten by anything, but they do like to bark. So after Cathy had come out to see the badger, I shut the dogs in the shop adjacent to the garage, turned out the garage light, and went to bed. Along about 4:30 I woke up and thought I'd better let the dogs out. Darned if the badger wasn't still in the corner under the ladder. I poked him with a broom handle to make him leave, but he just hissed and growled and looked mean. So I hit him with a stream of water from the garden hose and he waddle-ran right off into the graying morning. What he was sticking around for I don't know. Maybe he liked to hear our dogs bark.

Badger fights were a staple of Great Plains recreation in earlier days, a means both to initiate a greenhorn and to entertain the veterans. The way they often worked was that a promoter would come into a town with a badger in a barrel, a curtain over the open end, then take bets from the locals on whether or not any of their dogs were good enough to go into the barrel and bring him out. I remember John Hogoboom telling of a man who beat one of these traveling attractions. This was down in the oil fields of Butler County, at Midian or Oil Hill back in the 1920s. This little feist dog didn't look like much of a fighter, so the owner got a pretty good bet up on the deal. Then he threw the poor mutt into the barrel tail first, John said, and the dog came yelping out, the badger firmly clamped onto his rump. The badger let go and went running back into the barrel as soon as he saw daylight, but the dog sure enough brought the badger out of the barrel.

Then there was the snipe-hunting version of the badger fight, such as the one in Wichita back in 1914. Some sports at the Livestock Exchange found a tenderfoot who had never seen a fight between a badger and a dog, so while somebody rustled up a likely canine, a couple of others brought out a "badger" in a barrel, one end of which was covered with a gunny sack. Betting was spirited, with some of the perpetrators talking up the fierceness of the dog and others touting the invincibility of the badger.

In the meantime, however, some tender soul had reported the impending cruelty to the local humane society, and before the fight could commence a number of police officers showed up. The most officious of them, refusing all explanations, pulled on the rope attached to the "badger" and jerked out a bundle of rags, to the great amusement of the spectators.

The officers didn't take the embarrassment intended for the tenderfoot at all well. Three ranchers, getting ready to leave the stockyards on a streetcar and still chuckling over the incident, unfortunately within earshot of one of the irritated officers, were arrested for disturbing the peace. One of the cattlemen, an Oklahoman, wasn't overly pleased by the strict interpretation of Kansas law: "This is the first time I've ever been arrested for laughing," he complained as he paid his fine.

23. *Cold-Jawed Horses*

(August 1990)

A FEW weeks ago my son, who has been working on a ranch in the Flint Hills this summer, was telling me about doctoring some calves for pinkeye, work he particularly enjoys because it means swinging a rope instead of a hayhook. Josh was roping off of a big red roan that I bought as a yearling ten years ago. After a family council we decided to call him Zennor (registered names—in Roany's case it was Joetta's Big Boy—are usually either unwieldy or silly, in this case both), after a village on the Land's End peninsula where we all had been earlier that year, back when I was trying to track down the ultimate ancestor of the cattle guard—which happens to be the flat granite stile of Cornwall. When we got home that summer we did a little horse trading and ended up with a couple of nice colts, both roans, one blue and one red.

Now Zennor is a pretty good old horse—while not the best I ever owned, certainly not the worst—but he has grown up to be a good sixteen hands high and I've gotten to where I like a horse I can get on without jumping for the stirrup or else trying to find a ditch to lead him into or a tree stump to stand on. So I sort of willed Zennor off to Josh, who was building up his string of working horses.

Only Old Zennor wasn't working all that well that particular day—he can be just a touch temperamental. Actually I guess you could say that he's a little like a mule—he looks after himself first and worries about doing what you want him to do after he figures out that what you want is not going to hurt him. That morning he lined up on the first calf just fine and stayed right with him. On the next one, however, Roany decided that he was tired and kept veering off to the left so that Josh nearly wore his arm out pulling the horse back onto the calf. After the old cuss found out it wasn't doing him any good to misbehave, he went back to working right on the rest of the calves, his case of situational cold-jaw cured, for the rest of the afternoon at least.

Sometimes Zennor (or Turbo, as he got nicknamed on the ranch where Josh worked) would combine a cold jaw with a cold back, especially in an arena. He never bucked in a pasture, at least not hard enough that I can recall him doing it, but a few years ago when the Steuve boys were putting on weekly team ropings out west of Olpe, he'd insist on trying to hump up the first couple of times you'd take him out of the box. Sometimes I'd even ride him the eight or ten miles to the pens and he'd still have to act like he'd never seen a roping chute before.

One July night three or four years ago, early in the evening before they'd turned on the arena lights, he broke in two about thirty feet out of the box, bucking pretty good about three-quarters of the way down the arena. I got through that storm in good shape (nothing spectacular; probably would have marked somewhere in the high fifties), but I was so damn mad that when he quit bucking I started spurring hell out of him and wrapping him good with the rope. Big mistake. About the time I was reaching back across from his left hip to brand the right one with the nylon, he stuck his head down again and veered left. I went right.

After I got my wind back and the dirt knocked off my pants and the horse caught up, the problems were over for the rest of the evening. Zennor was through acting up and we had a pretty decent night on the heads.

Is there anything more aggravating than a cold-jawed horse? Or more dangerous, if you're heading for a tree or a fence or a cliff? Back in the late 1960s we raised a dark brown colt that turned out to be a pretty good team-roping and cow horse, but he gave me a few thrills when I was breaking him. We lived in Columbia, Missouri, at the time. I was in graduate school there and Cathy and I had leased a pasture four or five miles from town so we could run a few steers and have a place to keep our horses. We hauled Hector over from the Flint Hills the spring he turned three, and I started riding him. He never did buck and was coming along real well during the summer, so when we went to gather the steers to sell them in the fall I thought I'd ride him instead of Old Buck. Another big mistake. This pasture was hilly with lots of trees and a stream running through it. There was a cave at the base of a hill in the middle of the pasture with a good flowing spring that emptied into the stream. I don't know how far back the darn thing went, but that cave was big enough for all fifty steers to get into at one time. They liked to stay cool and get away from the flies. Or the roundup crew.

We had them on the hillside heading up into the pens, when a little bunch decided they'd rather be back in the cave. I took out after them, but instead of turning with the steers when they veered down the west slope of the hill, Hector kept going straight—right for the steep bluff bordered by a line of trees overlooking the cave. Pulling back on the bit didn't slow him down at all, and when I pulled on the right rein and brought his nose back against the stirrup, he still kept running straight for the edge. To this day I couldn't tell you how we missed taking a twenty-foot dive into the four inches of cold spring water that flowed out of the mouth of that cave. I don't think it was anything I did, but somehow the horse turned and I finally got him stopped.

But my near miss was nothing compared to one of my favorite cold-jaw stories. Charlie Russell told it. Lots of people don't know that he could sometimes paint with words nearly as well as he could with pigment. This story was about some cowboys who were riding the Missouri breaks country in central Montana. Along with the regular hands that day was the horse breaker, who was putting some miles on a green-broke colt. Now I don't know that country from horseback at all, but I have driven through it a time or two, and I do know that what looks like fairly level land as you're driving along suddenly turns into deep gullies and steep cliffs as you get closer to the river.

Everything was peaceful enough until the bronc rider decided to have a smoke. The colt didn't pay any attention when the cowboy pulled out his bag of tobacco and rolled a cigarette, but when he reached down to strike a match on the button of his chaps pocket the horse blew apart. At the start the rider was more interested in educating the colt than he was in stopping him from pitching, so he stuck the spurs to him and started quirting for all he was worth, determined to take the orneriness out of the colt once and for all. He was so intent on administering the lesson, in fact, that he failed to notice that the horse, who was bucking out straight, was headed right for a cliff. By the time he saw what was happening and started pulling up on the horse's head, it was too late. As the plunging horse neared the edge, the cowboy's companions quit their whooping and hoorawing and watched in awe as horse and rider headed out, and down, into space.

I don't remember how far Russell said the drop was (and I sure don't vouch for the truth of this tale), but it was far enough that a big cottonwood tree growing at the bottom of the gully didn't show up from where the cowboys sat on the tableland a few hundred yards away. They loped their horses to the edge of the cliff and looked over, I'm sure with a fair amount of trepidation in their hearts. There was the colt, unharmed, perched in the top of the cottonwood, with the bronc rider, unharmed, still firmly in the saddle, his unlit cigarette in his mouth. When his companions hollered down to see if he was hurt, he twisted his head up and around back toward them and called out calmly, "Toss me a match. Mine went out on the way down."

Conventional cowboy wisdom holds that a cold jaw is caused by using a harsh bit on a young horse's mouth—that's what Jack Thorp says, in *Pardner of the Wind,* where he particularly damns the Mexican ring-bit—but I think some equines are just born that way. And are gray horses more likely suffer from the condition, or does it just seem like it? The two most exasperating cold-jaws we ever owned were gray, one a nice-looking gelding that Dad traded for back in the fifties and another that we bought as a yearling several years ago. You needed a bull rider's arm to manage either one, especially if they got a little hot.

Cold-jawed horses aren't all bad, though; in fact they're real good for providing entertainment for other cowboys. Jay Young, a friend since boyhood who has spent his life working on the TZ Ranch near Cassoday, had a big old bay horse that he used a special long-shanked hackamore on—unwrapped bicycle chain over the nose and a piece of small log chain under the jaw, but even that often wasn't enough. The horse had some good qualities, but stopping on cue was not one of them. On calf-roping nights at Ralph Rohmeyer's arena you could always count on at least one runaway from old Bay Tide. One time, Dad told me (I wasn't along that day), Jay was helping to round up a two- or three-section pasture out east of town. A couple of steers started toward daylight, and Jay ran them back into the bunch. And then he just kept right on going, right through the middle of the herd at full speed, scattering cattle everywhere, pulling and cussing and yelling "whoa" all the way to the east fence a mile or more away. He finally traded the horse off, but only after years of putting up with him.

As I said, Bay Tide had some good qualities, as many of these cold-jaws do, I suppose, but still you wonder, after you finally get rid of one, why you kept the damned old thing around as long as you did. Maybe it's because they look good or are easy to catch or will work real well for weeks on end— until something upsets them and they take the bit in their teeth. Or maybe it's simply because a cowboy just hates to admit that any horse might have a bad habit that the cowboy can't train him out of or persuade him to quit. But it can be pretty hard to make a lasting attitude adjustment on a horse that has been cold-jawing off and on for most of his working life.

Not long ago I was talking to Glenn Brewer of Elkhart,

Kansas, whose father had owned some land bordering the Stonebraker Ranch in the Oklahoma Panhandle. One of the horses on that ranch was bad about cold-jawing and would, when the reins were pulled, throw his head back along his side and keep on running. Just imagine being on top of a horse running full speed with his head on your knee and looking you in the eye instead of at the rocks, cactus, and prairie-dog holes ahead. This horse had once run away with a terrified fourteen-year-old girl, going several miles before he tired enough so that the ranch hands were able to catch up with him and rescue her.

Only one cowboy, employed to ride fence on the ranch, could handle the horse. When the pony would cold-jaw and throw his head around the way he did, this old cowboy would simply meet him in the middle of the forehead with a hard swing of his saddle hammer. After a few sessions of this type of Pavlovian training, the horse gave up his runaway habit and would dutifully lope mile after mile of fence, stopping right on cue whenever the cowboy pulled on the reins.

Brewer told me, "I still ride where the Stonebraker cowboys rode, but not on a cold-jawed horse." Sounds good to me. Life's short enough as it is without getting into a contest of wills with a cold-jawed horse—or human.

24. *Longhorns on the Anchor D*

(October 1982)

RICHARD, ROBBINS, JR., of the Anchor D Ranch in Kansas has been in the Texas longhorn business only since 1975, but longhorns are as much a part of his family heritage as is the Robbins name. Dick's great-uncle, Edward D. Robbins, shipped longhorns from Texas to a Kansas feedyard before the turn of the century. The elder Robbins, a Kansas rancher, had acquired an interest in some land in Reeves County, Texas, part of the old Hash Knife outfit, sometime around 1897 or

1898. Along with the land came a herd of longhorn steers, ten loads of which Ed Robbins decided to ship to his feed-yard near Runnymede, Kansas.

The steers were unloaded at Norwich, a few miles from Runnymede, accompanied by some Texas cowboys and cow ponies. The Texans had only contempt for the Kansas cowboys, part of the Robbins crew that had been sent to help. "Nesters on plow horses is what they thought they were," Robbins told me.

"In those days a good trail boss rode ahead of the herd with a pocketful of nickels to give to little boys so that they would tie up dogs along the route," he said. Unfortunately, this trail boss didn't think about farm wives and their gardens. The steers were headed for the pens at a trot when suddenly a woman came running out of her house, apron flapping. The steers scattered everywhere, and the Texans found out that they were not so well mounted after all. In fact, the Kansans on their "plow horses" were much more effective in gathering the spooked steers.

Even with Texans and Kansans cooperating, they never found all the steers, and the longhorns that did get put in the feedlot never completely settled down. Dick Robbins's father, Richard Whitfield Robbins, who was eight at the time, remembered in later years that he and the other kids got paddled several times before they learned to stay away from the pen with the Texas cattle. "The same man, wearing the same clothes, had to feed them at the same time every day, or they'd go off their feed or break out," Robbins said. "The cattle never did get fat; they just got bigger. I don't think Uncle Ed came out too well on that deal."

Maybe not, but these particular steers became famous in another way, serving as the model for Frederic Remington's painting "Texas Longhorns in a Kansas Corn Corral." And today, longhorns still are a part of the Robbins ranching operation, where they are looked upon with greater favor by Robbins than were those troublesome creatures acquired long ago by his great-uncle.

The Anchor D today runs commercial herds of Hereford

and Angus cattle and registered Texas longhorn cows on
some thirty thousand acres in Kiowa County and four thousand acres in Pottawatomie County.

Robbins had heard that longhorn bulls threw small calves,
so in 1975 he bought two bulls (Chain Ranch Quixote 80 and
WR Ranch 3290) and two WR heifers. He still has them. The
longhorn cross, like the Jersey, produced a small calf at birth,
but as the calf grew it put on some size. As Robbins said, "It
looked like it was a real member of the cow family." In 1976
he went into the longhorn business seriously, buying ten
heifers from Darol Dickinson. He still has seven of those
cows. He also has cows that he bought in 1977 from the WR
herd. Robbins likes longhorns for more than their small
calves, however. "The heat doesn't bother those bulls," he
said. "An Angus bull will go lie in the shade on a hot summer
day, but those longhorns keep moving. And they will boss a
herd just like a mustang stallion will herd his bunch of
mares." Robbins keeps around fifteen bulls on his herd of
registered cows.

A few years, ago, while doing research for a book on the
history and lore of cattle guards, I sent a questionnaire to
Dick Robbins. In his response, he told me about seeing, on
the Anchor D Ranch in Oklahoma, the date 1912 marked in
the concrete foundation of a cattle guard. I mentioned that
response to Robbins when I visited him recently, and asked
him about the Anchor D and why he chose it for his brand.
His reply: it's a good, clear brand that can be read from a
distance. From what I could tell, he also chose the Anchor D
for personal and historical reasons. He was raised on that
ranch, living there from his birth in 1942 until moving to
Pratt with his father in the mid-1950s. The original owner of
the brand was Charles Edward Dudley, a Boston whaler who
had to leave the sea for health reasons. He moved to the
Great Plains, our nation's sea of grass, where in 1868 he first
burned the Anchor D into cattle. Some say the brand was
really just his initials run together, but most think that he was
homesick for the ocean and the brand was a reminder of the
old days—an anchor combined with his last initial.

Another link with history in the Robbins operation is the present ranch headquarters, located on the old Frank Rockefeller ranch northeast of Belvidere. Frank was a brother of oil tycoon John D. Rockefeller, and he lived on the ranch off and on during the 1880s. There are a number of the original buildings left, including two very impressive barns. The horse barn, complete with single stalls and wooden floors, is built of wood and native stone, quarried several miles to the east. It is a cool barn, just right for the Anchor D's twenty head of mules and about twice that many horses. Several sets of harness hang at the ends of stalls, evidence of Robbins's enjoyment of driving mule teams in parades and of his use of mules to pull feed wagons during bad winter weather.

The other barn is one of the longest I have seen. It was Rockefeller's bull barn, Robbins told me, and inside I saw dozens of wooden tie stalls. "Rockefeller tried to operate the way they did back east and in Europe, where they brought the cattle in every night. He had every bull brought in and tied up at night. And then he wondered why he didn't get a very good calf crop!" Rockefeller also kept some buffalo around. Along with C. J. "Buffalo" Jones of Garden City and Charles Goodnight of the Texas Panhandle, Rockefeller probably helped keep the bison from becoming extinct.

You can pick up some interesting bits of range lore hanging around Robbins. "A slow learner often retains," he said, "whereas an easy-broke horse can be screwed up just as easy, but one that you have to drill it into will usually get it right and remember it."

"When I was in the army, we had to hurry up, then stand in line and wait," he recalled. "I hated it, and so do cows. When we work calves, I get the laziest or the slowest guy and put him back behind. We run the calves in one chute and the heifers in another for pregnancy testing. That way we keep a steady stream going without making them stand in the chutes and getting them impatient or nervous."

I asked him if his longhorns were spooky or gentle. "Any animal will be spooky if you push it. I remember Roy Beedle [an old time Flint Hills cowman from Bazaar] saying, 'Don't crowd, don't crowd the cattle. Dammit! Well, get on your horses and go bring 'em back!'" Indeed, the Robbins long-horns were gentle, as I discovered when we went out to pho-tograph them and I walked around and among them, snap-ping away.

Riding around with Dick Robbins is not only a fine way to spend a day, but also a history lesson in ranching on the central plains. The Robbins family came to this country in the 1630s in the second wave of settlers, arriving in what is today Connecticut. They apparently did well in agriculture (Dick Robbins has an 1854 Robbins Company seed catalog out of Weatherfield, Connecticut). William W. Robbins (Dick's grandfather) came to Kingman County, Kansas, in the early 1880s, where he was followed shortly by his brother, Edward D. (who had the troublesome longhorns mentioned earlier). The two brothers formed a partnership and in 1887 put to-gether the ranching operation near Belvidere in some of the prettiest grass in the West, part of the same country that Dick runs longhorns on today.

In 1915 William Robbins died and Edward D. bought his interest from the estate. After World War I, Dick's uncle, Edward C. Robbins, went to work for *his* uncle, Edward D., managing the ranch at Belvidere. The elder Robbins died in 1932, and Edward C. continued to manage the estate for the next several years. In 1935, Dick's father moved to Kansas and formed a partnership with his brother, thus creating what might be considered the second stage in the history of the Robbins ranch.

The brothers leased all the land in the estate of their uncle, as well as leasing the neighboring Bean Ranch. They bought the Palmer Ranch north of Belvidere, the Rockefeller Ranch northeast of town, and the Hall Ranch in Comanche County. They also leased the Anchor D Ranch in the Okla-homa Panhandle, near Guymon. In 1941 they bought the Moffitt Ranch on Diamond Creek in the Flint Hills of Chase County, Kansas. Because of the prolonged drought, as well as for health and personal reasons, the partnership was dis-solved in 1956, but Richard, Sr., continued to expand, buying the Nesbitt Ranch between Trail Creek and the Yellowstone River in Montana. (This ranch was sold in the mid-1960s.)

Richard Robbins, Sr., (Yale 1913) was raised by "three Puritan old maid aunts," one of whom received an M.D. degree in 1878. "Aunt Jane was probably one of the first women doctors in the country," Dick Robbins told me, "but in the Spanish American War, and in World War I, she had to serve as a nurse."

Dick's father was not only a rancher, but a man of importance in business circles. In 1930 he put together three smaller airlines, thus forming, and becoming the first president of, TWA. In March 1941, at the age of forty-eight, he was elected to the board of the Santa Fe Railroad, its youngest member. For some reason, he had to miss the October meeting that year, and when he walked into the November meeting the chairman of the board greeted him, more than a little sarcastically, with "Howdy, stranger." It so happened that one of the major items on the agenda that month was a train wreck near Fort Sumner, New Mexico, that had killed a huge number of sheep—thirty carloads were part of the train that derailed.

When the meeting reached that point, the Chairman said something like, "Well, we've got a real problem here, a wreck that killed some farmer's sheep."

"I know," said Richard Robbins. "Those were all my sheep." From that point on, Dick said, his father had no trouble whatever with any Santa Fe officials about his attendance at board meetings.

When I asked Dick just how large the Robbins brothers' operation was, he had some pretty impressive figures. In 1952, the largest year, the Robbins ranch ran seventeen thousand head of mother cows over two counties in Oklahoma and eight counties in Kansas. Dick has a 1938 map of the Belvidere ranch alone that shows the east-west dimensions marked "one-half day's ride" and the north-south "one-day's ride."

Not only was the operation large, it was diversified. Besides having, at one time, the nation's largest herd of short-horns, the ranch also produced seed sorghum, hogs, sheep, and even turkeys: "From eggs—for eating or setting—to chicks to breeding stock to dressed birds."

The Robbins ranch also had raised horses during the army remount program of the 1920s and '30s. The army supplied the stud—a good one—and they reserved the right to buy any or all of the colts up to age three. One year the Robbins brothers sold eighty-five head of horses to the army. The trouble, from the cowhands' point of view and from that of the ranch owners, was that the army always took the best horses. The ranch paid its hands a dollar a day extra to break colts, which had to be given at least thirty rides in ninety days to get them ready for the army to inspect. Some of these horses had developed into excellent cow horses, and the hands hated to lose them, so they developed a few tricks to fool the army's horse buyer.

Dick Robbins remembers a visit a few years ago from an old-time army horse buyer, who asked him why so many otherwise good Robbins horses got turned down for un-soundness. Robbins had learned the answer from his father years before. The cowboys would rub a sore just above the horse's hoof with a piece of rope. The horse would limp, and he had what looked like a scar, but it was all temporary. Within a few weeks the hand would have his favorite mount healthy again and safe from the army's clutches.

The latest stage in Robbins family ranching history began in 1964 when Dick Robbins began ranching on his own, seven years before his father died. "I started out in Pot-tawatomie County when I was twenty-two years old. I grew up in the ranching business, and when I was a kid I kept a notebook and would write down things that worked around a ranch and things that didn't." This youthful experience was gained, among other places, on the Anchor D Ranch in Oklahoma—"Until I was ten years old, I thought Texas was a county in Oklahoma." Robbins spent the summer of 1959 working on the Montana ranch owned by his father and the next two summers on Robbins land in the tallgrass of Chase County, Kansas.

When I was growing up near Cassoday in the Flint Hills of northeastern Butler County, I often heard of the Robbins ranch from friends who had gone to Belvidere to work there. I knew it was big and a good place to work, but I had no idea that there was so much history and tradition attached to the operation.

25. *Pringle Ranch Longhorns*

(April 1983)

DICK PRINGLE of Yates Center is a friendly, outgoing man with the forthrightness someone from the eastern states might expect of a Kansas rancher. When he talks about longhorns, he smiles. "They're my motorboat," he says. I look a bit puzzled, I guess. He goes on, "Other people have motorboats or fancy campers for fun. I have longhorns."

Indeed, he does have longhorns and has had them longer than anyone else in this part of Kansas. He bought his first cows in 1966 (three of them from the Blair Ranch near Atlanta, Kansas, one—now twenty-seven years old and still going strong—from the YO Ranch), well before the Texas longhorn breed became a popular or commercial success.

While Pringle is not a major longhorn breeder, neither is he just dabbling. He has a herd of thirty-five or forty high quality cows (built up by keeping heifers from his original purchase), a few aged steers (ranging from sixteen to nineteen hundred pounds, each with an imposing set of horns), and a young registered bull. He sells the purebred, but unregistered, heifers and bulls at about eighteen months of age, getting around nine hundred dollars for heifers and up to fourteen hundred for bulls.

Many cattlemen have eased into longhorns by starting with a longhorn bull to put on first-calf heifers. Although Dick didn't start this way, he soon learned the value of the practice. He is now exclusively using young longhorn bulls on the replacement heifers for his seven-hundred-head commercial cow herd. In this, his main operation, he likes Brahma-cross cows, with Hereford bulls on the mature mothers for an animal that will feed out efficiently. Since 1971 Dick and his wife, Mardelle, have put their cattle, plus some they buy, into their own one thousand-head feedlot a mile or so southeast of the ranch house. The Pringles own and lease over twenty-five thousand acres, including the historic Nuttle Ranch in the Flint Hills near Rosalia. They raise all their hay and much of the grain used in the feedlot, as well as some cash grain crops.

I went to the ranch just south of Yates Center to visit with Dick a couple of weeks before Christmas in 1982. I'd have gone a bit earlier, but he was in Chicago, attending a meeting of the Beef Industry Council. In fact, while I was talking to the Pringles in the feedlot office, Dick was waiting for a Council conference call. When it came, I talked to Mardelle for a while, learning the extent of Dick's involvement with the bureaucratic side of the beef business.

"Dick was president of the Kansas Livestock Association, back in 1979, I believe," she told me. "He's also a member of Farm Bureau, the Texas and Southwestern Cattle Raisers' Association, the National Cattlemen's Association, and the Kansas Texas Longhorn Association. He's a board member of the National Livestock and Meat Board and was cow-calf chairman of the National Cattlemen's Association a couple of years ago."

All this work for the industry must keep him pretty busy, I remarked. Mardelle agreed, and Dick told me later that he probably spends a quarter to a third of his time on industry business, including travel. In the past couple of years he has made official trips to Chicago (seven or eight times), the West Coast (twice), Idaho, Nevada, Arizona, and a dozen trips to Washington, D.C., especially when beef legislation is pending. He is quick to give credit to the Texas Longhorn Breeders Association of America (along with other purebred associations) for its support of a one-dollar increase in registration fees to finance beef promotion.

Mardelle is active in her own right, besides traveling with Dick to many of the livestock meetings. She served a term as president of the Kansas CowBelles in 1978 and is currently National Membership Chair. And what does she think of raising longhorns?

"Well, at first I was against it. It seemed like we were spending money without any chance or intention of getting anything back. But you know, some years during the 1970s when nothing else was breaking even, those longhorn yearlings were the only thing we sold that made any money. And, because we keep them along the highway, they do get us some attention."

Not all of that attention was positive, but that was the fault of the buffalo, not the longhorns. Dick bought a bison bull and cow from a nearby zoo several years ago, and he put them in with his longhorn herd. "People kept stopping to tell me that a buffalo was on the highway, or the sheriff kept calling," Mardelle recalls. "So Dick finally sold him—it was the bull that kept getting out." Interestingly, the bison bull and cow never produced a calf, but once the bull was gone, the cow became pregnant by a longhorn bull.

"The cattalo is a fairly uncommon cross," Dick told me as he was tossing some alfalfa to the herd while I took photographs, "but see that one over there? That's a calf out of the cattalo cow and a longhorn bull. That kind of a cross is not supposed to happen, but it did."

Mardelle likes the longhorns now, except when they get out and come up to the house. "They like to shine their horns by rubbing them on my shrubs and bushes. They've broken every tree I've ever planted." So she keeps a broom handy to run them off with, but doesn't harbor any grudges.

The Pringles have three children, all of them, like their father, graduates of Kansas State University. Kent, the oldest, is an attorney in Chanute, while Todd, the youngest, is a broker in the Chicago Mercantile Exchange. The middle child, Beth, worked for the Monsanto company for a few years after graduation (in 1979), and she has now returned to the ranch, working alongside the half dozen or so other hands usually employed there.

Beth is as capable with a horse as she is with a four-wheel-drive feed truck. While her father was talking to the other members of the Beef Industry Council, she drove me to a nearby pasture to see some young longhorn heifers. On the way we passed a small group of yearling bulls. "Those are for sale," she told me. "All our bulls are fertility tested before we sell them." Beth lives a mile west of the feedlot on the old home place. And that old home place is, in a way, the reason Dick Pringle first bought longhorns.

"Longhorns are part of my heritage," he told me. "My grandfather raised them in Arizona back in the 1880s and sent some back to this country to be pastured on bluestem, then fed them out on corn. My grandmother's parents lived back here, and they would herd the longhorns on grass owned by the railroad or they'd put them on leased grass in the Flint Hills north of Eureka. Then they'd put them in a feedlot of sorts, a feeding barn, and fatten them on ear corn.

"When my dad was a boy, it was his job to keep corn shoved into the feed chutes and to break the biggest ears in two so the longhorn steers could eat them. It wasn't a very efficient use of feed—at least until they started running hogs in behind the steers. I feed Brahma-cross cattle in this feedlot now, but the first cattle ever fed in this part of the country were longhorns."

I asked how his ancestors got into the cattle business.

"Well, my grandfather and two of his brothers came to this country from Scotland. The oldest brother, you probably know, was the one who inherited the land in those days. The others weren't destitute or anything like that, but they did have to do something to earn a living."

One of those things, I learned, was freighting supplies by ox and mule train from the Mississippi to Arizona Territory. There, in the 1880s, they managed to work a deal with the United States whereby they were given the right to run cattle on government land, so long as they sold the cattle to the government, primarily for distribution to reservation Indians and to the army. "You remember that television series 'High Chaparral'?" Dick asked. "That was the same sort of country and operation that my grandfather and great-uncles ran."

The government contract specified that there would be a 15 percent cut on all cattle delivered, no matter how uniform the herd was. That's where the longhorns came from that were shipped by train back to Kansas for grazing and feeding.

Eventually, his grandfather decided to move back to Kansas. "Things were getting a little too rough in Arizona," Dick said. "Indians weren't a problem, but the white settlers were. A lot of them weren't really settlers; they were ruffians, outlaws. One of my great-uncles was killed in a barroom shootout with a rustler. I still have a longhand copy of the trial record. They convicted the killer, but my grandfather decided to move back anyway."

Mardelle told about going to a National Cattlemen's Association convention in Phoenix in 1981 and stopping in Globe to see what they could of the Cherry Creek Ranch, which was run by the Pringle brothers a hundred years earlier. "A lot of people at Phoenix read our name tags and asked about Cherry Creek," she said.

Dick said the brand he uses today, the Flying H, came from his grandfather and was the first ever registered in Arizona. "It was supposed to be impossible to alter with a running iron, but somebody thought of extending the legs of the H, then connecting the wings to make a big dollar sign."

"They began to get quite a bit of mining in that part of Arizona," he continued, "and they had to pump water up and over the mountains and back into the mines. We went to see the Pringle Pump, a station built nearly a century ago and still standing.

"You know, it's interesting. A hundred years ago my grandfather raised longhorns in Arizona, and now I've got a friend in Flagstaff who tells me that they are going back to longhorns there because that's the most profitable breed for that part of the country. There's some rough land out there— seven or eight cows to a section where we can get a hundred or more back here—and longhorns do better on it than anything else. We've gone a full 360 degrees."

Dick leaned back in his chair. A plaque of a longhorn (the logo of his ranch, appearing on everything from wooden gates to stationery) hung over his head; a Wanda Johnson print of some longhorn cows in an Arizonalike desert setting was to his right. The smile crossed his face again.

"This is not a fancy outfit. I don't have any show cattle. I just have a few longhorns because my grandfather had them." Deeply committed both to the heritage and to the future of the cattle business, Dick Pringle recognizes both the romance and the practicality of the longhorn.

26. Wild Cattle

ABOUT three years ago a friend was telling me about helping ship some wild cattle from a pasture in southern Chase County. He said that a dozen cowhands (both men and women) had worn out two or three times that many horses, not just trying to get the cattle into a set of shipping pens, but literally trying to get them out of the pasture where they had been summered. Coincidentally, a couple of weeks later I was talking to another friend who was regaling me with stories of trying to ship a pasture full of wild cattle. I thought at first that he had been in on the Chase County roundup, but this pasture, he said, was east of Cassoday in northeastern Butler County. It was part of the Vestring Ranch and had been filled with cattle from south Texas.

Recently Bob Vestring told me the story of that roundup. The cattle, he said, were from the Jones Ranch near Falfurrias, a ranch that apparently has developed a reputation for wild cattle, even in Texas. These steers, which would run at the sight of a horse, had been rounded up in Texas by helicopter. In their summer pasture in Kansas they didn't see many horses, either, and would run if they saw a pickup driven into the pasture. So when September came and it was time to ship, Bob assembled a crew of hands who were well mounted and knew how to handle cattle. I forgot to ask just who all was helping, but one man he did mention was Bud McLinden, who has probably looked at as many cattle from the back of a horse as anyone active in the Flint Hills today.

There were something like four hundred head of these steers, but after a full day the crew had managed to get only about a third of them into the pens some half dozen miles away. Most cattle are gregarious and will bunch up, that is, come together and stay together when they are moved. But these steers went off in every direction as soon as they saw the horses. And if you got close to them, they would charge the horse. Or else they would throw their heads and their tails up and run to the far end of the pasture—and then keep on running. They jumped fences like steeplechase horses. The running didn't bother the Brahmas among them, but a couple of the Herefords died from heat stress. One cowboy was injured and a horse was permanently lamed.

A couple of days later, and after another try (they got about sixty head this time), Bob called a man named Payne of Webb City, Oklahoma, who had a reputation for owning good cow dogs. Payne's dogs had been used on outlaw cattle from Florida to New Mexico and he guaranteed success. But the Jones Ranch steers scattered just as much for the dogs as they did for the cowboys—two hundred steers running two hundred different directions, six of them with dogs dangling from their tails or their muzzles.

After that it was back to the cowboys, some on horses, some in pickups, some on three-wheelers. It took three weeks to get the last steer caught and shipped. The final thirty or forty were roped and dragged into stock trailers one at a time—some of them miles from the pasture.

Now I can just hear Dad or Uncle Marshall (as representatives of the old timers) snorting over the superiority of their own methods and abilities over today's cowboys and their horses, but I'm not so sure. At the 1992 National Cowboy Symposium in Lubbock I listened to Slim Vines of Crane, Texas, tell about some wild steers he had worked with in the

1930s, and the only difference between then and now seems to have been that the steers back then were four times as old and three times as big. The ranch Slim worked for had bought some cattle in Mexico, so wild that many of them had to be roped and yoked up to oxen to be brought into the pens. He talked of big old steers clearing seven-foot fences without touching them. He told of roping a twelve-hundred-pound steer on a nine-hundred-pound horse on a dry lake bed, then skidding along for yards and yards after he made his catch, waiting for someone else to get there and get another rope on the steer so they could stop him. He laughed about the foreman warning the hands to watch out for a particular stub-horned steer: "Hell, no need to warn us. We were watching out for all of them all of the time!" After all sorts of trouble they finally got the cattle into the pens at El Paso and from there to the ranch in west Texas. The next spring they shipped the steers to the Flint Hills for summer grazing, then on to market. "Those cattle were so wild and skittish," Vines said, "that they actually weighed more at El Paso when we first brought them over the border than they did a year later at the Kansas City stockyards."

Slim Vines didn't know about the difficulties that Flint Hills cowboys might have had in getting these Mexican cattle onto the cars in Kansas, but I'd be surprised if they were much easier to handle than the ones Bob Vestring pastured during 1990. I can't help but wonder how the old-time drovers would have handled cattle like these. Probably no better than their twentieth-century counterparts. But at least the old longhorns often ran together when they stampeded, or would break off in bunches, not scatter off each one a different direction. Besides that, the old longhorns were used to the sight of a horse—they hadn't been chased out of Texas by helicopters.

Part Five

WORK

27. *Burning Pasture*

Only a Kansan would consider an annual burn-off of the
prairie.

—J. R. and Sharon Hamil, *Return to Kansas*

YOU'VE heard all the songs—"Springtime in the Rockies,"
"Apple Blossom Time," "April in Paris"—but I don't think
that anyone who has ever driven the Kansas Turnpike at
night from Emporia to El Dorado during April will forget
springtime in the Flint Hills. Small-plane pilots on their first
Topeka–Manhattan or Kansas City–Wichita nighttime hops
have been known to ask, "Is the world on fire?" Out-of-state
motorists, stopping at Strong City or Council Grove to report
what they think are uncontrolled range fires, are often heard
to mutter words like "Armageddon" and "Holocaust." What
they are actually seeing is an annual rite, a traditional agricultural practice, a folk custom of Flint Hills range management known in the vernacular as "burnin' pasture."

Agricultural burning is an age-old practice; slash-and-
burn is still a major method of ground-clearing in many
Third World countries. In America, intentional range burning (the result of Indian and British influences) was carried
out in colonial Georgia and the Carolinas at least a half-
century before the Declaration of Independence.

The custom had spread to the trans-Mississippi West by
the early 1800s, but by the end of that century it was encoun-
tering popular opposition (probably part of the general
farmer-rancher contention of the times). Range burning fell
into disfavor with twentieth-century agricultural scientists,
many of whom were vocal in their opposition well into the
1970s. Some of this opposition, both popular and scientific,
might be attributed to the Smokey-the-Bear syndrome: forest
fires are bad; therefore, all fires are bad. Only in the last
decade have range management specialists begun to swing
the pendulum back, to convince both farmer and public that,
properly used, prairie fire can be a very good thing indeed.

How good? According to Paul Ohlenbusch, range management specialist with Kansas State University and self-pro-
claimed pyromanager, fire is the cheapest, most natural way
to improve grass quality, increase livestock gains, cut down
on weeds, brush, and trees, and increase wildlife vitality.
Ohlenbusch has been preaching the pasture-burning gospel
for nearly two decades: "Fire does the same thing herbicides
and mowing would do, only a heck of a lot cheaper. Besides,
if you want to burn, you have to leave enough grass in the
pasture in the fall to burn in the spring. That means that you
don't overstock—which means healthier grass, more gain on
livestock, and less soil erosion."

Ohlenbusch's contention that wildlife benefits from range
fire is seconded by Roger Wells, Kansas Fish and Game agent
stationed in Emporia. Prairie chickens, for instance, prefer
freshly burned pastures for eating and booming, second-year-
after-burning pastures for nesting, and third-year or more for
cover. That is why, according to Ohlenbusch, there are more
prairie chickens near Cassoday (which calls itself the Prairie
Chicken Capital of the World) than around Matfield Green
or Bazaar, fifthteen miles to the north. Huge areas of pasture
there tend to get burned every year, while at Cassoday pastures are burned less often and more selectively.

Other wildlife also responds well to burning. Quail, for
instance, may lose their nests in a pasture fire, but they will
renest. They produce fewer eggs on the second nesting but
end up with the same number of young birds in the fall—and
these young tend to be bigger and stronger than their first-
nest cousins. Burning doesn't do much to discourage grasshoppers; some varieties will feed on freshly burned pastures,
others on those not burned. The main adverse affect is on
rodents that like the thatch of an unburned pasture.

With advantages like these, why would anyone oppose pasture burning? Ignorance, mainly. Except for Flint Hills
ranchers, nobody (the general public, other ranchers and
farmers, agronomists) understood range fire or realized its
benefits. As Pete Maley, Lyon County agricultural extension
agent for three decades, put it, "Back in the 1950s if you had

put a match to a pasture, I'd have strung you up from the nearest utility pole." Maley is now an advocate of fire. Retired Wabaunsee County agent Darold Marlow also knew that pasture burning was supposed to be bad, but he had some lingering doubts, especially when the ranchers near Eskridge and Alma had such excellent grass. So he just kept quiet and let them burn.

Norman Schlesener, former Kingman County agent, came along a bit later. By the time he was graduated from K-State in the 1960s, the official line was changing. The ecology movement, which on one hand strengthened some of the popular opposition to pasture burning, on the other hand caused range management specialists to realize that the tallgrass prairie could not be maintained in its native condition without fire.

And fire is something that Flint Hills ranchers continued to use, from the 1870s through the early 1900s, when other Americans quit burning, through the 1930s, when other Kansans quit burning, and right on up to the present day, when ranchers all over the country are being encouraged to start burning again.

According to Ohlenbusch, only in the past dozen years has fire regained acceptance—and only in Kansas did the practice of pasture burning linger on, a hundred-year outlaw. The only major improvement over the folk method during this hundred years, in fact, has been the scientific finding that burning is more beneficial in late April or early May than during the traditional month of March.

Ohlenbusch's colleague, range management specialist Clenton Owensby, is another strong advocate of controlled burning. Owensby, one of the foremost researchers on range fire in the world, left the Forest Service in New Mexico to come to K-State in 1967, largely because officials there (Smokey's home state) disagreed with his ideas that fire could be beneficial. "Kansas has been in the forefront of controlled burning throughout the century. [R. L.] Hensel, in 1918, and [A. E.] Aldous, in 1934, [both K-State scientists] were the first in the country to publish research on pasture burning," Owensby told me recently.

Today pasture burning is being practiced in many other states, but Kansas is still the leader. Here in the tallgrass we burn, intentionally, 1.5 million acres annually (soon to be 2 million), and not just in the Flint Hills. U.S. Highway 77 used to be the western boundary of the pasture-burning area, but now burning covers nearly two-thirds of the state. Ranchers in the Gypsum Hills near Medicine Lodge have been burning to control cedar trees since about 1979, while burning in Kingman County has been going on since the early 1980s. Down in the Osage country of Oklahoma, as well, burning has increased in the past couple of decades.

Don Mecklenburg, overseer of the 108,000-acre Cimarron National Grasslands in the far southwestern corner of Kansas, has burned a couple of thousand acres a year there for the past ten years or so. The grasslands are home to possibly the best assortment of wildlife in the state—blue and bobwhite quail, lesser prairie chickens, pheasants, turkeys, mule and whitetail deer, antelope, elk, and an occasional bear— and Mecklenburg thinks that the burning helps not only the grass but the animals as well.

There is a strong traditional belief, backed up by at least some evidence, that Indians used fire to attract game. Plains Indians were known to burn the plains as a weapon—scorching the earth in order to deprive their enemies of fodder for horses. They also apparently knew that game would be attracted to the new grass that followed a fire, a definite advantage in the days before they acquired the horse.

A transcript of an interview from Emporia State University's Flint Hills Oral History Project with the late Jerry Moxley, well-known Council Grove livestock breeder, illustrates the folk belief of Indian burning:

> The reason the Flint Hills are such a great grazing area was because of the treatment the Indians gave this land. They burned the grass each spring. They would burn it this way: the squaws would weave a large ball of this long-stemmed bluestem grass and then the men would take their braided rawhide lariat rope and would throw it around those bales or balls of grass. They would put their lariats on each ball

of grass, and they would set it afire. Then they would ride just as far as they could go with that ball of fire and set the grass afire. The reason they burned it was to bring the buffalo in; they liked fresh green grass so this area was noted as a grazing area for buffalo.

Contemporary pasture burning in the Flint Hills is a bit more mechanized. Marjorie Handle, in the centennial history I edited for my hometown in 1984, describes it well:

> Burning the pastures in the spring is an adventure. It takes a lot of backfiring so you don't burn the whole countryside. This is done by having three trucks full of gas so you don't get stalled somewhere. The first truck sets the fire along the fence with a sack of fire or a welding torch. The second truck with a sprayer full of water follows close behind to put out the big fire while the third truck comes along and puts out the little fires, like cowchips or posts that are still burning. You do all this when the wind is in the right direction and hope it doesn't change before you get the whole pasture burned. It helps if several pastures are burned at the same time.

Both of the foregoing methods are preferable to what Paul Ohlenbusch calls the "coffee-shop burner." This guy sets fire to one side of his pasture, then goes to town to drink coffee and gossip while the sirens of the local rural fire district go blaring past. By the time the fire is stopped, it has reached the other side of the section and he has gotten his pasture burned at the taxpayers' expense.

The old-fashioned way of burning pasture was best described to me by Ben Scharplaz, who lives southwest of Minneapolis, Kansas, in the Smoky Hills. Scharplaz (who loves grass as much as I do, but has a heck of a lot more of it to love!) was born in Switzerland in 1910. He came to Kansas when he was nine, settling in Ellsworth County with his mother and sister. After a stint in Louisiana (and except for a summer making hay in Montana in 1932) he moved back to Kansas for good in 1927, working on various ranches in the Ellsworth-Saline County area.

Scharplaz remembers that there was a lot of pasture burning in the Smoky Hills at that time, but that the practice died out in the later 1930s as a result of pressure from the Agricultural Soil Conservation Service. He kept right on burning, however, and when he moved to his present ranch in Ottawa County in 1957, he induced several of his new neighbors there to give it a try. They are now believers.

Among other things (such as carpenter and cabinet maker) Scharplaz is an artist, and one of his paintings shows clearly how pasture burning was done back in pre-automotive days. His painting shows one man driving a team of sorrel mules hitched to a wagon loaded with two barrels of water, a pair of bib overalls hanging over the top rim of one barrel. Two men are on foot in front of the wagon. The first one is pulling a garden rake through the burning grass, setting a line of fire as he goes. The second man has a bucket of water and a pair of soaked overalls and is beating out the backfire line. They have almost reached the southwest cornerpost in the pasture, an unburned pasture to their backs and a pasture burned a few days earlier (as revealed by the slightly lighter shading in color—an excellent bit of realism) to their left.

Scharplaz told me that his painting is based on how they used to burn pasture when he was a youth working on the Gregory Ranch in eastern Ellsworth County. They often burned at night when the wind was down. Bill Gregory would tell his hands after dinner, "Well, boys, you might as well go to the bunkhouse and rest this afternoon. We'll burn tonight." They would start at sundown, a community effort with several neighbors helping out, often working until midnight before they had the periphery completely burned and could go to bed and let the inner grass burn itself out (sometimes a day or more later).

Scharplaz told me that he liked to use bib overalls with the suspenders cut off, not gunny sacks, to fight fire. "You could slaughter fire way better with a pair of overalls," he said. "They are a lot heavier and have a solider weave. You don't have to soak them up as often and you don't have to stoop over the way you would with a shorter sack." Two men would always work a fire together. The lead man would knock the fire with the overalls, always being careful to hit straight with the fireline or toward the burned area; hitting toward the unburned grass could knock sparks into it and start more fire. The follower would hit the small fires left in the fireline and kick smoldering cowchips into the burned area, minimizing the possibility of their restarting a blaze. The two men would trade positions when the leader got tired or needed to resoak his overalls in the water bucket.

"I always liked working with horses," Scharplaz told me, but soon Model A pickups had replaced the mules on the water wagon at pasture-burning time, just as now four-wheel-drive pickups, mechanized water sprayers, and CB radios have become standard pasture-burning equipment. The burning grass itself, however, is a link with folk custom, and with the past, that can't be changed, no matter how mechanized we become.

Of the many different things I have smelled in my life, I find few more pleasing, more clean than the springtime smell of distant smoke from burning bluestem grass.

28. *Pasture Roping*

SOME OF the greatest roping catches ever made have occurred not in a rodeo arena or on a vaudeville stage (remembering Will Rogers) but way out in the middle of a remote pasture, often unwitnessed and, like the poet's mute Milton buried in a country churchyard, unsung—unless the roper is the sort of fellow that is unencumbered by modesty, false or otherwise. Uniformity of conditions (or more precisely the lack of it) is the reason that catches in a pasture are often more spectacular (if generally slower) than those in an arena. Contest ropings take place in a fenced-in area of relatively small size with a smooth, level surface, whereas every pasture has its own unique terrain. Moreover, indoor arenas, some of the more fancy of which are heated in winter and air-conditioned in summer, remove even the weather as a variable.

Coping with rain, temperature extremes, and wind can definitely affect your aim. Another area of uniformity is in the rodeo stock itself—calves and steers are required by PRCA rules, and by accepted usage on the amateur circuits, to be within certain weight limits, and they must be replaced if they begin to go sour, (the roper's term for calves that duck and dodge or steers that won't drag right).

But in a pasture you have to rope whatever needs roping whenever it needs it—baby calf with screwworms, mother cow with swollen bag, ringy bull with wandering eye, cantankerous yearling with foot rot. And usually wherever you find it. Even if you should manage to maneuver the ropee onto a flat, smooth section of pasture to start your run, he will invariably end up in the roughest brush and rocks by the time you catch him. And it's the rocks and the brush—and the draws and the trees and the badger holes and the cattle guards—that create the excitement and the spectacle of those pasture catches that rarely find equal in a rodeo arena.

A while back, for instance, one of our neighbors here south of Emporia was chasing a heifer down a fencerow, just about ready to make his throw, when for no good reason she made a sudden turn through the wire. The typical mindless yearling-heifer kind of thing to do. His horse, trained to follow, made the same sharp turn but stopped dead at the wire, thereby transforming Willie into a hood ornament for the saddle horn. But it turned out okay. Somebody else caught the heifer, and Willie was walking halfway normal again in only a few weeks.

Sometimes fences simply provide an interesting obstacle to the roping. One Flint Hills cowboy told me of catching a wild steer just as it leaped over a low stone corral wall, his horse leaping over the same wall as he pulled the slack. It was pure luck and bravado, he said, but it mightily impressed a visiting New Mexico cowboy who had just unsuccessfully chased the same steer.

Another pasture-roping exploit that sticks in my mind was performed by the late Raymond "Peanuts" Prewitt back around the mid-1950s. Peanuts was one of my idols when I was growing up, a tall laconic man with a ready laugh, and a hell of a cowboy. Besides having a cow herd and summer-pasturing Texas steers, he and his wife, Melba, kept a stud horse and raised good colts, lots of them. Melba could train a horse to do anything but sit on its hind legs and talk, and Peanuts could darn sure make one work cattle. They had both rodeoed, Melba as an RCA trick rider and Peanuts as one of the best calf ropers and bulldoggers—and wild-cow milkers—in the amateur rodeos held throughout the tall-grass region. Melba had retired from the arena when the kids (four eventually) began arriving, but Raymond was still going strong as I was coming of age.

He roped and dogged off a little brown mare that hardly weighed a thousand pounds, but she was quick and fast and well trained. I used to go down and practice roping calves with Peanuts, and more than once I've seen him ride into the box, slip the bridle off and hang it on the fence, then turn the mare, set her, and rope a calf. Betty Jo, he called her. Named after an old girlfriend, he'd say, and wink at Melba. Gave her (the girlfriend) up when he found out that she was going out on late dates after he had taken her home. The mare obviously had a whole lot more character than did her namesake.

Oh yes, the pasture-roping exploit. I didn't see it, but I heard of it and when I asked Peanuts he grinned sheepishly. He was checking his cows one day, he told me, and there was one, a Hereford that would weigh over 800 pounds, that needed roping. He put the mare on the cow's tail and whipped his loop around her head and pulled the slack. Then, "I knew I shouldn't have done it, but the ground was smooth and the cow was ornery and the horse was working good. I signaled Betty Jo to stop, and she shut down, tucking her hind legs under her, and jerked that cow head over heels, just like she was a 250-pound calf."

My first attempt at heading and heeling, which took place over a quarter century ago when team roping was just begin-ning to spread out onto the plains from the Southwest, was a classic example of pasture-roping mayhem. Doug Todd, a

Outlaw steer in the Santa Fe stockyards at Cassoday, 1938. (Author's collection.)

Two Flint Hills cowboys. Kenneth (*left*) and Marshall Hoy, c. 1935. (Author's collection.)

Kenneth (*right*) and Marshall Hoy, a half century later, 1986.
(Author's collection.)

good friend and shirttail in-law (his brother H. L. married
my sister Rita) from Rexford, out in northwestern Kansas,
was staying with us for a few days in the early 1960s. We were
between rodeos, I suppose, and Dad had us out riding pastures. I remember that it was summer and the grass was high.
It had rained the night before, so we were checking to see if
lightning might have hit a cow. And we were hoping that one
of the calves might have pinkeye, screwworms by that time
having been nearly ruined as a reason for roping, thanks to
the big eradication program down in Texas.

Hell, it was even better than we had hoped; there was a
stray yearling in with the cows. He didn't have pinkeye and he
didn't have foot rot, but neither was he ours. And we could
tell just by looking (being possessed of an intuitive power
that is especially strong in younger cowboys) that this steer
would have to be roped in order to get him back into his own
pasture.

But first a necessary digression about our mounts, particularly mine. I *think* that Doug was riding his calf-roping
horse, but I *know* that I was riding Old Buck (and he could!).
Only he wasn't Old Buck at the time because he was young,

about a five-year-old. Now Buck was a good, big (1,250 pounds
with the saddle after a hard day's work), heavy-muscled red
dun. He was out of Rusty, one of the best cow horses Dad ever
had, sired by Sutherland's Fire Hair, a cutting horse that
Wayne Rogler was standing at the time on his ranch near
Matfield Green. Dad had given him to Rita when he was
born, and she called him Travis. But then she got married
and moved off and the horse grew a big cyst just above his
right eye and they had to have him hauled up to the vet
school at Manhattan to get it cut out and then it grew back so
we got the local vet to cut it out and it didn't come back, but
the eyelid always drooped and the tear duct always flowed so
Rita sold him to me. Things didn't seem too promising at this
stage of his life, but Buck turned out to be the best cow horse
I ever owned; he was big and stout and quick and agile and
could see more cow with his good eye than most horses ever
saw with two. He could also see out of his bad eye, enough to
spook, that's for sure. I had broken him to ride the winter he
was three, a winter with lots of snow, which made it easier to
steer him into snow drifts and slow him down when he
started bucking. Which he did with some regularity until he
was close to ten years old. A naturally suspicious nature,
combined with the wariness occasioned by hampered vision
on his right, gave Buck (I had changed his name to Claude
when I bought him from Rita, but it didn't stick—I ended up
calling him Buck or, with less sensitivity, One Eye) a tendency
toward jumpiness, of both the shying and pitching varieties.
A pitching sich and sich, as Texas cowboy poet Paul Patterson
might call him.

Anyhow Doug is probably the one who came up with the
notion of heading and heeling this steer. H. L. and Rita had
moved to California about this time and the reports H. L. was
sending back about team roping were whetting his younger
brother's appetite. So we both cinched up and took down
our ropes and tied them to our saddle horns. The ropes were
grass—I don't know if I'd even seen a nylon rope in the Flint
Hills at this time. The only dally roping I'd ever seen was at
the ribbon roping or wild-cow milking contests at the Coun-

tryman Rodeo. I take that back—my grandfather never tied on. But then I hardly ever remember seeing him with his rope down. Dadhoy had an old, nickel-horned, high-backed, wide-forked, Frazier saddle, the leather worn away on the front of the right swell where he carried his rope, but I can recall only once seeing him chase and catch a calf, the end of his raggy manila dallied around that slick horn. Doug might have seen some dallying out there in western Kansas, but at this time we were both roping the only way we knew how, tied hard and fast.

I figured to try the heading, so we cut the steer away from the cows and pointed him toward open country. I built to him and laid out as good a head catch (he didn't have horns) as I ever threw, before or after. Doug was right behind, rope swinging. Talk about explosive excitement! Buck chose the precise moment I jerked my slack to break in two. The bronc ride was going in one direction, the steer was running in another, but Doug was so intent on throwing his very first heel loop ever that he didn't even consider my predicament. He just rode in and threw. How he managed a perfect toss through foot-high bluestem on a steer that was being dragged by a runaway bucker I'll never know, but Doug caught both heels and his calf-roping horse set the brakes. By this time I had kicked out of the right stirrup and was leaning off to the left, ready to bail out if the horse went down, but when the ropes drew taut and Old Buck felt the jerk, he kept his footing and quit pitching. When the dust settled, we had that steer stretched out pretty as could be. Not the smoothest overall run we ever made, but the result was one to remember. At least the steer remembered it; he stayed where he belonged the rest of the summer.

One of the most impressive pasture roping stories I have heard is about a Chase County cowboy whose rope broke when he caught an old cow. This cowboy never even slowed his horse but, at full run and in less than a minute, coiled up his rope, tied a new honda, built a loop, and caught the cow again. Or so I was told by the man who claimed to have seen it. Did it really happen? Darned if I know, but it shows why pasture-roping stories are invariably good ones—the cows tend to get meaner, the rocks rougher, and the spills more colorful the farther the storytellers get from the pasture.

I don't want to give the impression that pasture roping is invariably spectacular, however. Actually much of it is routine, even dull if the animal needing doctoring is too sick to put up much of a struggle. Roping can get boring for even the avid roper under such circumstances. It happened to me during the fall of 1961 when I was riding for Wayne Rogler. Rogler had taken in several hundred head of Louisiana or Mississippi yearlings for wintering and had turned them into the Frue pastures on the county line, about six miles south of his headquarters near Matfield Green and a couple of miles east of the old Fluke house where I was baching. Bad weather came early that year, lots of damp chill in late October and wet snow throughout November. Those southern cattle, weak from the truck ride anyway, got sick by droves. Now Rogler, in common with many ranchers, didn't like to see a rope on your saddle, much less one swinging in your hands, but with these steers he had no choice. I was sent out every morning with a horse in the back of my pickup and a load of penicillin and glucose in the front seat, doctoring the sickest ones and cutting brands off the dead ones. For once in my young life I had all the roping I could handle, dozens a day. The two green horses they gave me to ride, a brown thoroughbred named Pockets (short for High Pockets) and a little sorrel quarter mare called Mary Ann, both three-year-olds, got pretty good at tripping and holding. It lasted a little over a month, then I quit and went to the rodeo at Chicago. I don't know if the pasture work actually helped the arena performance, but I roped a couple of calves there quick enough that I didn't have to take a regular job the rest of the winter. (Of course coon hunting didn't take much money, the way I did it, and gasoline was cheap in those days.)

Like Rogler, ranchers with an antiroping bias often enjoy watching roping at rodeos. They just don't want the hired hands out there practicing in the pasture—too many chances for injury to cattle and horses. Today, with the increased use of portable pens, there isn't as much need for pasture roping as in earlier years. Stock trailers have also caused a change in technique for pasture ropers. No longer does a sick animal have to be left in a pasture to endure repeated doctoring (and roping). Instead it can be roped once, dragged into a trailer, and taken back to the barnyard for some bovine intensive care. A well-executed piece of trailer roping, by the way, is a thing of beauty. If all goes well, the cow is run a short distance, caught near the trailer, the rope flipped over the stockrack (if it's an open top), and the animal dragged inside almost before she knows what has happened.

Another specialized form of pasture activity is moonlight roping, often indulged in (before the advent of stock trailers and portable pens) by rustlers. This type of roping was also practiced in earlier decades by high-spirited young cowboys out on the town. One of the stories I have heard my father and uncle tell is about riding home from Cassoday one moonlit Saturday night with the Plummer boys (or maybe it was the Sturgeon twins) and deciding to do a little moonlight steer riding, which in turn called for some moonlight roping. They caught one of the neighbor's cows easily enough, but in the confusion the rope horse ran off, dragging the cow for several hundred feet. She wasn't seriously hurt, but she did have a big patch of hair rubbed off her shoulder and side. A few days later the owner was in town, puzzling over the strange quirks of Kansas weather. It seems that one of his cows had been struck by lightning and had had the hair burned clear off one side but it didn't even kill her. Dad said that he and Uncle Marshall sat there without saying a word, knowing that *they* probably would have been killed if the owner, or Dadhoy, had known what really happened.

When I was growing up, we had around the house a photograph Mother took during her first year of marriage, a picture of an outlaw steer that Dad and Uncle Marshall brought into the stockyards at Cassoday in 1938. I remember Dad telling the story behind the photograph a time or two, but Uncle Marshall could spin a better tale. Here's his version of events:

The Teters were bringing in a bunch of cattle from out east of town, Greenwood County, and this one old renegade gave them a lot of trouble, a big old Brahma steer with tipped horns. He must have been a four- or five-year-old. They choused him around and finally got him across the tracks, but they couldn't get him into the pens. Your dad and I were hanging around the yards, and when that steer jumped the fence and headed north old Jim Teter asked us if we thought we could get him in. Heck, we thought we could do anything. So we called home and told Dad to get in the truck and drive up Highway 13. By the time we got within sight of the steer, he was already across the county line, three or four miles north in the east Frue pasture, heading down into a little canyon. I told Kenneth to come in behind him while I loped around to the far side so I could rope him when he came out. He ran with his head up, so it wasn't very hard to catch those high-set horns. [But then Uncle Marshall never had much trouble catching anything.] Kenneth roped his heels and we tied him up. By that time Dad was there with the truck, but there wasn't any good place to load him, so we had to drag him a couple of hundred yards to the nearest ditch. Dragging him on the grass like that burned the hair off his shoulder just like a brand.

When we got back to the yards, somebody asked us how we were going to get him turned loose—he was fighting mad. Dad drove into the big pen on the northwest and Kenneth tied the rope on the steer's horns to a post and hollered at Dad, and he drove out from under him. While he was still bouncing with all the wind knocked out of him, I jerked the rope off his horns and his feet, then jumped up on the fence—along with everybody else. Old Jim Teter started griping about how rough we were treating his steer, but I just told him, "What the hell are you complaining about? Your cowboys couldn't even get him into the yards."

I wasn't born at the time all this happened, and the stockyards have long since been torn down. But I have a copy of that photograph hanging on my wall, and when I look at it I can smell those old yards and feel the excitement. And I think of those two old cowboys, one of them now gone and the other in a rest home, and I think of all the horses they broke and all the cattle they roped. A woman who lived in an oil camp north of El Dorado told me not long back about how she remembered them, as young bucks, riding for Wilbur Stone. They would ride on the fender of a car as they were going past the local farms on their way to the pastures and rope chickens, which her mother would then cook for them.

Uncle Marshall was a really good roper, in both pasture and arena. I think that he pretty well summed up the typical cowboy attitude toward roping in a story he told me a couple of years before he died. He and Wilber Countryman were helping to move some of Stone's cattle from El Dorado to Rosalia, riding along at the rear of the herd and tossing their ropes at weeds and fence posts. Wilber was itching to cut one out of the herd and rope him. "What if the boss comes along?" asked my uncle. Wilber didn't even hesitate: "Why, we'll just tell him that we saw a steer that we thought needed roping, but after we got him caught we found out he didn't so now we're turning him loose."

29. *Counting Cattle*

SOME ITEMS of cattle-country wisdom I learned from my father: leave a gate the way you found it; don't miss any cattle when you gather a pasture; always be sure of your count. Some related wisdom I learned on my own: some gates, once opened, are damn hard to close; some cattle, if they don't want to be gathered, can hide behind a tumbleweed; some cowboys can count cattle better than others.

You know who the good counters are in an outfit, just like you know who the good ropers are. But it seems to me that whereas the fair-to-middling roper will usually defer to the man with the hot hand if a calf or a steer needs catching, nearly everybody in the pasture figures he can do just as well, if not better, than the two men at the gate doing the counting. Especially if one of them is the absentee owner or a commission man or some other outsider who is not part of the rank and file who have just gathered the pasture.

Counting is one of the more important aspects of the cowboy's job, especially here in the Flint Hills where the pastureman is responsible for seeing that every head he received in the spring is accounted for in the fall, with live bodies or with brands cut off dead ones or with piles of this year's bones. A pastureman never misses a chance to count his cattle, and he also keeps a pretty sharp eye out for the brands he's looking after in the pastures that border the grass he's got leased. But cattle counting transcends the pragmatic, goes beyond the purely practical consideration of having to pay for missing steers at the end of pasture season. It's one of those benchmarks of cowboying, a rite of passage that separates the kid from the hand.

I learned to count cattle by riding our cow pastures. Dad rented a half section a few miles south of our home place and we had other pastures scattered around closer in the other directions, each holding a part of our cow herd. At least once a week, oftener if there had been a rain with lightning, we would ride each pasture to check the salt, the windmill, and the count. So many cows, so many calves, and a bull or two. It was reasonably easy to do, and good practice for when I was older and got to helping with some of the big pastures in the Flint Hills east and north of Cassoday and west and south of Matfield Green.

There's one major reason to count cattle and that's to see if you've got all you're supposed to have, but the need for knowing occurs in several different situations. For instance, you have to know exactly how many cattle you're going to be responsible for during the grazing season, so you want to get a good count of the cattle as they come off the truck and into the pasture. Or if the truckers happen to dump them off before you get there, then the first thing you do is get a count on them in the pasture. Now it's reasonable to assume that the owner counted them onto the trucks when they left his ranch, and it's also likely that each truck driver knows how many head he has on his rig, but the smart pastureman gets his own count. That's not being suspicious; that's just good sense. Because if your count doesn't jibe with what was supposed to have been shipped, then it's easier to wrangle out the discrepancy with the owner in April than it is in October.

I remember once talking to an older cowboy who was looking after grass on the Butler-Greenwood county line in the early 1920s, before the railroad came through Cassoday. The cattle he was receiving had been shipped into DeGraff, about twenty-five miles west of the pastures where they would graze for the summer. The pastureman met the herd a few miles east of the Walnut River, where it had been penned for the night about halfway from DeGraff, and was told that they were all there, that the count was right. But he ran his own count, a couple of times, as they trailed east, and he was short 3 head. The foreman of the delivery crew scoffed and made light of the pastureman's counting ability, but when he insisted (with some little vehemence and no little profanity) that he wasn't going to be responsible for 500 head (let's say, for the sake of illustration) when there were only 497, the foreman sent a couple of hands back to search the brush around the river. There, in a little milk-cow pasture, they found 3 head that had somehow gotten out of the holding pen during the night. At least that was the foreman's story, although the pastureman told me that he thought those 3 head were really intended by the foreman to be his own little bonus.

On the whole most cattle owners are honest about the count, and so are most pasturemen. But I remember one pasture owner who was so suspicious that he caused a minor stampede. I was helping drive a bunch of southern heifers from a pasture about ten miles south of Cassoday where they had spent a few months of the summer. The farmer who owned the pasture was getting so much per head per day, but he didn't know exactly how many cattle were on the grass, and neither did the pastureman, because these were the damnedest cattle you ever saw to do anything with. They weren't wild, but they wouldn't drive, and you simply could not get them to string down a fence to get them counted. So when we finally got them out of the pasture (it took over an hour; they were leery of gates, too) and headed north up a gravel road, the pasture owner hopped in his pickup and gunned around the section to get in front of us, then drove up through a field to the fence about midway through that stretch of road. Instead of staying in his pickup and counting as best he could, he got out and crawled through the barbed wire and hid in some plum bushes on the other side so he could count as they went past. Everything was fine as long as he stayed hidden, but when he stepped out to thin out the string of heifers as they passed, they went wild. Some bolted ahead, some went through the fence on either side of the road, and the rest turned tail and started running as hard as they could back to the pasture they had just left. It was mayhem. Seeing as how I was hired just for the drive, I kept my cussing to myself, but I was damn sure doing some.

So you always count your cattle when they're delivered in the spring, and you try to count them in the pasture several times during the summer, about once every week or ten days. Pasture counting can be a little tricky, especially a big, rough pasture full of brush. Then, too, some cattle are spooky and will run as soon as they see a horse. Other times, particularly during the heat of the day, they'll be gathered into large bunches in the shade, fighting flies and trying to stay cool. The surest way to count a pasture is to round it up and string the cattle down the fence to count them. But that might well require the expense of a few hands, as well as running off some of the gain. So most cowhands will get to a pasture either early in the morning before the cattle begin to bunch up at the ponds or under the trees, or else in the evening, when the cattle begin to wander out into the cool. That way you can get a pretty good count without stirring them up too much. A couple of weeks just prior to shipping, however, the pastureman goes for an especially good count. That way he can hunt strays, if necessary, before the delivery date, at which time he might have to pay for the shortfall.

Most mid-season counting is just to make sure you have your count, but occasionally special circumstances arise. For instance, one Butler County cowboy told me of having to drive a banker through a big, rugged pasture so he could check up on his collateral. The cowboy thought the whole enterprise rather useless, especially when it became apparent that the banker couldn't have counted milk cows locked up in their stanchions. So the cowboy decided to help out. He would drive to the top of a hill, run a "count" on the cattle below, then drive along a ridge to the next bunch of cattle. He covered about a third of the pasture, told the banker that the count was right, and everybody was happy. It reminds me of the old open-range ploy of driving a single herd around and around a hill so that the greenhorn buyer ends up inspecting the same cattle several times over instead of seeing his entire purchase. A Chase County hand told me of the time a cattle owner had sent a Kansas City lawyer out to count the cattle in a four thousand-acre pasture. The lawyer got there about ten o'clock and drove around until noon, counting a bunch here and another one there. Then he went to town for dinner. When he came back to the pasture about midafternoon, he started counting where he'd left off, even though the cattle had done a lot of moving around in the meantime. That's one way to make sure you see enough cattle in the pasture.

Cattle usually get counted several times when you ship—a couple of times in the week or so ahead of time, once as they leave the pasture, another time as they are brought up in drafts to the scales, and again as they are loaded onto the pot-belly trucks. I remember one occasion when several hundred head of heifers were brought from a pasture in the Hills several miles east of town to the ranch headquarters west of Cassoday where they were to be pastured for a while longer before being shipped with some more of the same brand that had been grazing there all summer. Unfortunately, a bunch of them got out and several were killed by a train and others got scattered over a wide area. But just how many were lost was hard to tell because the pastureman had failed to get a count as they were taken from the first pasture, so he didn't know how many might have been left behind. As it happened, a good portion of the missing number were either overlooked in the first roundup or had strayed into neighboring pastures. The hands did a hell of a lot of riding that could have been avoided if there had been a good count to begin with.

There are all sorts of techniques to counting, and a protocol, too. Back when I was younger and helping with cattle more regularly, I could count with reasonable accuracy, as long as the individuals didn't bunch up too much as the herd went past. I tended, then, to count two at a time, which is less frenetic than counting singles. Counting by twos is, it seems, fairly common, but I've talked to people who see three or more at a time. Jim Young, one of the best pasture counters in the central Flint Hills, counted by fives, or so I've heard. I know that cattle could really string past him, and he never seemed to get flustered or behind.

This not being sheep country I don't have any firsthand knowledge, but I've heard that counting sheep is a real test of skill. Jack Thorp tells of sheepherders in New Mexico who couldn't read or count past ten. They would count pairs of sheep on their fingers, then cut a notch on a stick for each ten pairs. When the flock had passed, they would give the notched stick to the boss, who would count notches and multiply by twenty. Thorp said that these unlettered sheepherders could count flocks of several thousand sheep and not miss a single one.

Rather than multiplying, the old cow-country joke requires division: a cowboy is asked for the secret of his remarkable ability to count cattle. Easy, he says, I just count their legs and divide by four.

I've been told that the best thing to do when the cattle are coming hard and fast is to keep counting, to never stop even though you can't possibly be sure that you are getting every single head. This way, at least, you end up with a good estimate even if the count can't be relied on for total accuracy.

Most cowboys I know count up to a hundred, then start over at one, if the herd has more than a couple of hundred in it. The hundreds are often marked with an extended finger (three fingers and 48, for instance, means 348 cattle) or, particularly if there are more than 500 head, by tying a knot in the bridle rein for each hundred head. Or sometimes a cowboy will have a chaps pocket full of rocks and will transfer a rock to the other pocket for each hundred. Or he will take out his bullet-shaped commission-company pencil and make a mark on the palm of his glove, or on the saddle horn, or on a page from his pocket tally book every time the count hits the century mark.

Sometimes cattle are counted as they leave a pasture, but the disadvantage of this method is that because it is often hard to get cattle out of a gate to begin with, you don't want to take a chance of spilling them at the gate just so the counters can do their work. So sometimes the cattle, after they are rounded up, are driven down a fence line. The counters (sometimes only one, often two, if there are enough hands in the crew) will go to the head of the herd and let the cattle start stringing past in a narrow strip. Usually a couple of other cowboys will be there to narrow the herd down as it goes past the counters, to keep the cattle from going too fast, and to keep any from passing behind the counters as they face the fence where the main herd is stringing through. Each counter counts silently, sometimes moving a hand or nodding his head toward the cattle as they go past, and other cowboys in the crew are careful not to talk to or otherwise distract him. If one or more head do get behind the counters, then the other cowboys wait until the herd has been counted to inform them. Sometimes, when there is a break in the stream of cattle, one of the counters will call out his tally to see if his partner agrees. Or sometimes when the count hits a century mark, one cowboy will pinch off the flow and call out the tally to his counting partner. This helps keep things a little less complicated, especially on a large herd. Pretty much the same pattern can be followed in a large pen or when driving a herd down a road.

Whether or not you're selected to count cattle depends on where you fall in the hierarchy. Usually it's up to the cattle owner (if he's around) and the pastureman (or whoever is in charge of gathering a pasture) to count the cattle themselves or to designate a deputy. And there's a certain amount of status involved. I remember well the first time that Dad called on me to count at a roundup. I was in my teens and we were in Chase County shipping the Yoakem pasture, which Dad looked after for John Berns. When Berns asked Dad if he wanted to ride up front to get a count, Dad sent me up to do it. Although Berns had been polite to me before, there had always been that bit of (perhaps unconscious) condescension that a cattleman has for a kid. But my count agreed with his, and from then on I was accepted without question. The same thing happened a few years later when Wayne Rogler shipped one of the pastures that bordered the Yoakum and Dad delegated me when Rogler asked if he wanted to count and check for brands. I had ridden for Rogler before as a hired hand, but he had never thought of me as worthy of counting until then.

As I mentioned earlier, almost everybody in the pasture thinks he's a hell of a counter, although not everybody is. I remember one summer, I was maybe twelve or fourteen years old, when a cowboy from the Southwest spent some time in our area of the Flint Hills. As I recall, he was from Arizona—I don't know for sure—but I do remember that he always wore a black hat and that he had black chaps. He also liked to talk about all his wonderful experiences—and triumphs—as a cowhand. I don't know how good he really was, but he struck most of us as not as good as he thought he was. I'm not sure who he was working for, maybe Vestrings or maybe he was on the McGinness Ranch, but he was doing quite a bit of day work for Zebold and for Frank Klasser (pronounced *Clayzure*). Dad had ridden for Klasser for years, ever since he moved into the Cassoday country, and Klasser had a lot of respect for his abilities, so Dad often got called on to count the cattle out of the pasture as we headed for the stockyards a dozen miles away.

This particular day, Klasser was shipping eight carloads of grass-fat McCann and Welder two-year-old steers to the Santa Fe pens, which meant that we needed 224 head to fill the cars. Jake Jordan, the ranch foreman from Victoria, Texas, was there to do the cutting. My sister and I were holding the cut, the most boring job and therefore the one always relegated to kids, if any were available. After what seemed an interminable while, we looked up and saw Klasser, Dad, and Black Chaps riding toward us to count the cut. Now Black Chaps had been talking all morning long about counting cattle—about how he counted several thousand corrientes that crossed the border into Arizona and never missed a single head, about how he was the only cowboy on some big roundup in Texas to get an accurate pasture count on lord knows how many head.

Dad counted 224 (confirmed when the cattle went on the scales and into the cars) while Black Chaps was two short of that. Without hesitating, Klasser turned the main herd back into the pasture and headed the fats toward town. Black Chaps spent most of the drive talking, to anyone who would listen, about how bad the cattle had bunched up when he was trying to count.

Counting Cattle

To the owner the final payoff depends upon the weight,
But to the pastureman what matters is how many clear
    the gate.

He counts cattle all summer long, checking lightning kills
    and strays,
For if he's short at shipping time, then he's the one who pays.

Now counting takes a special skill, one not possessed by all,
But status also plays a part, and there's a protocol

In counting: don't ever ride between the counter and
the herd,
And keep the cattle coming smooth, don't let 'em get
too stirred;

String 'em easy down the fence, don't let 'em bunch
too tight,
And keep track of all that slip behind, so the tally
comes out right.

And, unless you're asked, don't presume to move up
to the gate;
Let the owner count, and the pastureman, or the men
they designate.

You'll know you've finally made a hand, worthy of full
trust,
The day the old man nods your way and says, "Why don't
you get a count for us."

30. *Shipping Cattle*

PROBABLY the most satisfying part of the working cowboy's
job here in the Flint Hills is shipping out the last load of
pasture-season cattle. Unless his boss has a good-sized cow
herd that has to be fed all winter, that means the cowhand
can spend the rest of the year on odd jobs: breaking a few
colts, patching fence, maybe taking care of some stockers
bought along during the winter. The cattle owner doesn't
always find shipping to be such a pleasant experience—
especially if he bought high and is selling low. But to the
hands, shipping brings a sense of completion, of resolution
to the annual cycle of cattle-handling here in the tallgrass.

Shipping cattle is fun—it was one of the great joys of my
boyhood. At least my memory now tells me that it was fun,
although if I think back beyond the nostalgia of youth long
past, I recall some distinct unpleasantness—riding for hours
without water on dusty, windy summer days with the tempera-

Texas cattle in the Santa Fe stockyards at Bazaar, 1921. (Photo courtesy of Kansas State Historical Society.)

ture above a hundred, getting up at 2:30 or 3:00 on rainy, chilly fall mornings to milk cows and catch horses that didn't want to be caught. But all in all driving cattle, no matter how many times you have done it, is an ever-new adventure. And it was even more adventuresome before possum-belly semis replaced trains as the major carriers of cattle.

In my young mind I didn't distinguish between shipping and receiving. Technically, the Flint Hills pasturemen at Cassoday would receive cattle (that had been shipped from Texas) in mid-April, then along about mid-July they would start shipping, usually to Kansas City or St. Joe, where the commission men would receive the cattle for sale. Shipping or receiving, we got to drive them whether they were going to or from the Cassoday stockyards (or the pens at Aikman or Matfield Green or Rosalia or wherever).

Kansas has been a major cattle-shipping center for more than a century, ever since the Texas-to-Kansas trail drives that followed the Civil War. Before the war Texans drove their cattle to ports such as Galveston, from which they were shipped to New Orleans and other markets. They also drove them overland to Missouri, Illinois, and other eastern states, as well as westward to the goldfields of California. These early drives, however, tended to be small and the markets somewhat uncertain. Also, there were road hazards—alkali deserts and Apaches along the California Trail, irate Missouri farmers along the Shawnee Trail.

The Shawnee Trail, cutting across the extreme southeast tip of Kansas, was the first major route to the eastern markets and the first one to be used after the Civil War. Those who remember the old "Rawhide" series on television might recall that Clint Eastwood, Eric Fleming, and Sheb Wooley were on their way to Sedalia, Missouri, not Abilene or Dodge City, with their herd. But the Missourians didn't like the tick fever that infected their cows after the immune longhorns had passed through the countryside, and the farmers made life tough for the Texas drovers—beating them up, tying them to trees and horsewhipping them, threatening them with gun and knife. So much for the stereotype of the peaceful farmer and the hell-raising cowboy.

The major Kansas shipping centers had their origins in Joseph G. McCoy's post–Civil War speculative venture at Abilene. After trying to build pens along the Kansas Pacific at Junction City and Salina, he was finally able to get the cooperation he needed at Abilene. Or maybe it was just lack of resistance—Abilene, with only a dozen or so buildings in 1866, was too small to protest.

McCoy was quite a promoter. Originally from Illinois, he convinced Kansas Pacific officials that if they put up money for stockyards, cattle would pour in by the thousands and the railroad would get rich off freight charges. All these promises from a man who didn't own a single head of livestock or have a single contract with anyone who did.

But he was right. In 1867, as the pens at Abilene were nearing completion, he sent a man down toward Texas to locate cattle owners and convince them to follow the Old Chisholm Trail to Wichita and keep on going to Abilene. As luck would have it, his emissary ran into a drover in Indian Territory who was grazing his cattle there because he didn't have nerve enough to head them across Missouri, where he had experienced some "unpleasantness" the year before. The Texan was glad to divert to the Kansas railhead and the rest, to adjust the phrase, is legend.

Abilene, the prototype of the cow towns, reigned as the premier cattle-shipping center in the nation for five years, loading out a million head before getting civilized and warning the drovers off in 1872. The Queen of the Cow Towns, Dodge City, was predominant during the later 1870s and early 1880s. Newton, "Bloody Newton," where upwards of a dozen men were gunned down in less than a year, reigned as the major cow town in 1871, with Wichita and Caldwell vying for the title during the mid-1870s. Other major nineteenth-century shipping points in Kansas included Baxter Springs (on the Shawnee Trail), Ellsworth, Brookville, Hunnewell, Ellis, Great Bend, and Hays.

By the latter part of the century, homesteaders, fence

laws, the blizzard of 1886, and lower freight rates in Texas had brought the golden age of Kansas cattle shipping to an end, but large numbers of cattle have never stopped moving into and out of Kansas. Elgin, a tiny border town in Chautauqua County, shipped more cattle than any other single railhead in the nation during the early years of the twentieth century. Most of these cattle came from the vast tallgrass pastures of the Osage country of northern Oklahoma.

Another major shipping point during the teens and early 1920s was Bazaar in the Chase County Flint Hills. In 1923–24 the Santa Fe extended its track from Bazaar on through El Dorado and the new cattle shipping center became Cassoday. For many years after that more cattle were shipped into and out of the stockyards at Cassoday than at any other set of Santa Fe pens, one reason for which was that the freight rate changed between Cassoday and Matfield Green so that it was cheaper to hire cowboys to drive cattle twenty miles than it was to ship them the extra distance by rail. I'm sure that many other small towns in other grazing areas of Kansas—the Smoky Hills, the Gypsum Hills, the Comanche Pool country of southwestern Kansas—could also lay claim to cattle-shipping glory; I just don't happen to know their names.

Thousands of cattle continue to move into and out of Kansas each year, not only to and from the pasture regions mentioned above, but to and from the many feedlots in the western half of the state as well. Since about 1960, this movement has been largely by truck instead of by train. Whichever way shipping takes place, however, getting cattle to the pens still requires a roundup, and in the tallgrass country of Kansas that means horses and cowboys.

31. *Waiting for a Train*

THE HISTORICAL trend has been to make cattle drives shorter and shorter. Before the Civil War Texans drove cattle to markets as far away as Chicago, a distance that the postwar Kansas cow towns cut in half. Before the turn of the century north-south railroads made it possible for southwestern cattle to be hauled to summer pasture in Kansas, after which they would be hauled on to feedlots in Iowa or Illinois or to slaughter in Kansas City or Chicago. Cattle still had to be driven overland to the railroad stockpens, however, sometimes a considerable distance.

In the 1950s trucks began to replace trains in transporting cattle, a process virtually complete here in the tallgrass by the mid-1960s. At roughly the same time feedlots began to be established on the High Plains and soon thereafter the packing houses also followed Horace Greeley's advice. As a result Finney County today has the world's largest meat-packing plant (the second largest, also an Iowa Beef Processors [IBP] operation, is here in Emporia), as well as several of the state's largest feedlots. About the only cattle driving left for many western Kansas or Texas Panhandle cowboys is to herd a pen of fats down a feedlot alley and onto a semi waiting to haul them to IBP. I suppose it won't be long before the feedlots are moved next door to the packing plants and a conveyer belt will move cattle directly from feedbunk to processing lines.

It's probably different in the mountains and on the big spreads of west Texas or Nevada, but in the major pasture areas of Kansas (the Smoky, Flint, and Gypsum hills), Nebraska (the Sandhills), and Oklahoma (the Osage Hills), cattle drives today rarely extend for more than ten or fifteen miles, usually much less. Semitrailer trucks often haul the cattle directly to pasture in the spring and load them out from portable pens in the fall.

Now, while I will admit that trucking cattle has a certain charm (truckers are often called—wrongly in my opinion—the latest incarnation of the mythic American cowboy) and many advantages (less work and thus less labor to be hired, easier on the cattle and thus less weight lost in transit), still it lacks the elan, the flair that shipping by rail had. I don't know why, but I've never explored the bed of a cattle truck—never even been tempted to, but I always liked to walk into the cattle cars along the railroad loading dock. The allure of cowboys and trains is a strong one, a combination of two of the most romantic folk images in our culture.

Maybe trucks are less romantic than trains because they are more convenient. Say you've got a pasture full of steers ready to ship to the feedlot. You call a trucker and tell him to be at the pasture a little before noon. Then about midmorning you haul a set of portable pens to the pasture, set them up, and round up the cattle. The trucks arrive, you load out, tear down the pens, and you're back home for dinner before the ice has had time to cool the tea.

I'll admit that's a bit of an exaggeration, but shipping by rail the way we did it at Cassoday back in the 1950s took much longer, was much harder work, and was a lot more fun—at least that's how I remember it. I was around seven years old, and my sister Rita five, when we first got to help drive cattle other than those of our father and grandfather. This was in the later 1940s when the cattle pastured in the Flint Hills were mostly two-year-old (or even older) Texas steers. Many of them weighed over half a ton, nearly twice what they had when first put on grass.

These steers would arrive in mid-April, some of them so weak and thin that they had to be tailed up to get them out of the cars. Smaller yards had only a pair of loading (and unloading) chutes, while larger shipping centers (such as Cassoday) had an open unloading platform that could handle several cars at once. Somehow or other it seemed as if the trains always arrived at three or four o'clock in the morning—cold, drizzly, dark mornings. Then, as soon as daylight came, the cattle would be driven to the surrounding pastures, sometimes up to twenty or twenty-five miles distant.

By mid-July (the goal was to have a load ready by the Fourth) these erstwhile thin, weak steers would have piled on the flesh and shipping would begin, a process that lasted all summer. Each week, usually on Sunday (so the cattle would arrive in Kansas City fresh for the Monday market), the cattle owner or his foreman or the commission man would select a few carloads of the fattest steers and we would drive them to the yards for loading (usually no more than twenty-eight steers would fit into a car that had held forty-four in April). By late August or September most of the feeder cattle were out of the Flint Hills, only the cow herds remaining on pasture until the mid-October end of the grazing season.

A typical shipping day for us began at three o'clock A.M., for we had to milk cows, feed calves, eat breakfast (usually pancakes and pounded-and-floured round steak—occasionally, if we were running late, Mother would make bread-butter-and-steak sandwiches for us to eat on the way), and saddle and load horses before driving a dozen miles east of Cassoday to be in Frank Klasser's Big Pasture by the time it was light enough to see the tips of our horses' ears. If the lights were on at the TZ Ranch as we drove by, we knew that the Youngs would also be in the yards that day—along with one or more of the other outfits in the area: the Prewitts, the Harshes, the Crockers, the Teters, the Vestrings.

Although some had to drive farther than others, the pattern was the same for all of us: round up a pasture and hold the herd on a hilltop or in a pasture corner while the market-ready steers were cut out and held a short distance away. Even as a youngster it didn't take me long to spot the hallmark of cattle that were ready for shipping—round globs of fat protruding on either side of the base of the tail. Someone would then count the rest of the herd back into the pasture (pasturemen never missed a chance to get a count), and the drive to the stockyards would commence.

The drive from Klasser's ranch ranged from twelve to fifteen miles, depending on which pasture we started from. There was a spring in the Harsh Hill Pasture about ten miles from town, the last chance for a cool drink until we hit the yards, unless, as she occasionally did, Mary Klasser met us at the Watkins Flat Pasture with a lunch—tasty homemade potato chips and beef salad sandwiches.

We came out onto the road after crossing the Flat Pasture, over half the drive having taken place across grass—the Mosby, the Turney, the Harsh Hill, and the Prewitt Hill pastures. The final leg of the drive went a mile and a half along the west side of Fox Lake (built in the early 1920s by the Santa Fe to provide water for steam engines), then west one mile to the stockyards. There, after penning the cattle, we would sort them into batches of twenty or so for weighing before returning them to pens to await the train.

And it was sometimes quite a wait. We would usually have the cattle weighed by early afternoon and then ride down to Opal Green's cafe for something to eat (Texas cattlemen as well as tallgrass cowboys will remember Opal for her thin-crust cherry pie, the best ever made). If the train didn't come in just as we were sitting down to eat, it wouldn't come in for hours—or that's how it seemed.

Once it did arrive, however, everything moved at the Santa Fe's command. Now I would hate to imply that the train crews were imperial or anything like that, but it didn't seem to me that they went out of their way to make things any easier for the cowboys. (Another advantage of trucks— truckers get right down into the pens with their hotshots and help load cattle.) Of course, the trainmen had begun their work early in the morning somewhere in the southern tall-grass, stopping at every set of cattle pens along the way until they arrived at Cassoday, and they still had to stop at Matfield Green and Bazaar before they could pull on to Kansas City. Loading cattle wasn't very exciting to them by the time they got to Cassoday.

I remember hearing about one incident during a night loading at Cassoday where a cowboy was complaining about the cars not being very well lined up with the loading chutes. The brakeman wasn't overly sympathetic and the cowboy offered to teach him some manners. Just as the cowboy jumped off the loading platform (about four feet high), the brakeman swung his lantern and caught him alongside the head, then jumped onto his chest and started punching. As the other cowboys gathered on the loading platform overhead, the cowboy (who had yet to throw a punch) hollered, "Get me away from this guy before I hurt him!" The brakeman couldn't keep from laughing and the fight ended. Thereafter he would say each time the cars stopped at the chutes, "Is that all right, cowboy?" "Close enough," was the reply, no matter how oblique the angle.

No wonder townspeople and farm families would often come out to the stockyards after church and Sunday dinner just to watch the cattle being loaded, as one woman told me they used to do at Volland up in Wabaunsee County. You never knew what excitement might occur.

Cowboys at Comisky, a loading station on the Missouri Pacific east of Council Grove, were among the few who never had to wait for a train. The siding there was slightly inclined and after penning and weighing the cattle, someone would climb aboard the cattle cars, loosen the brake, and let them slowly roll into position, then tighten the brake and stop the cars, repeating the process until all the cattle were loaded. Then they could go home and let the train pick up the cattle whenever it came through.

Most tallgrass cowboys, however, especially if they are over forty, have spent more than a few hours waiting for trains. My most memorable wait was in the fall of 1962, helping to ship some cattle that Neal Harsh had pastured.

We had the cattle weighed and ready for loading in the early afternoon, but the train didn't come in until five or six in the evening. Or maybe it was later. To tell the truth, I don't recall the actual time because some of us (including Richard and Jay Young) had decided to do our waiting at Bill's, at that time the one store in Cassoday that sold beer. But we heard the train as it whistled into town and we headed for the door.

Somehow or other we were short my horse; someone had already ridden it back to the yards. So I climbed up behind Richard on Old Mutt (an ugly-headed, washed-out sorrel that was a pretty good cow horse when he wasn't hot and sulling), both of us with long-necked Buds in hand, and we took out for the stockyards as fast as Old Mutt would run. Harsh said that as we were coming up the road all he could see was flying foam.

That was the last time I helped ship cattle from the Casso-

day stockyards and one of the very last times they were ever
used. They were finally torn down in the mid-1970s. Utility
and romance, unfortunately, seldom mix.

The Outlaw Steers

The cattle that now graze upon the grass
Of the Flint Hills are mostly yearling steers and heifers,
Tame and small compared to those that came
Up in the cars from Texas in springtimes past,

Aged steers, whose lanky frames filled fast
With the rich bluestem, transforming sun and rain
Into protein for the hungry in cities far away
From the pastures where we played at work under vast

Skies that seemed as endless as our days.
But, as our youth, so too the Big Beef Steer
Gave way, as had the longhorn of the open
Range, receding into memory's haze.

Through sequent waves of imperceptible change, I recall
A time when in my youth I saw, and touched,
A moment that divided past and future:
The last of the big steers, shipped out in the fall.

It was in the later fifties, two-year-old steers
Still filled the Bluestem, but tastes were changing,
And tender feedlot yearlings would soon replace
The heartier grass-fat beef upon the tiers

Of market shelves. And there had not, for years,
Been any of the four- and five-year-olds
My father and uncle yarned about, cattle
Driven miles from railroad shipping pens, and fears

Of blackleg, fever tick, and worse. But then one spring
Welder and McCann, combing the cactus and the brush,
Had shipped up from Victoria, in a herd of eight hundred
Head, three outlaws, steers that had taken wing

During previous roundups—some eight years, or ten;
They were big, these brutes, with an eye not wild but aware
And calculating, and Klasser, the pastureman, was worried.
How would he ever manage to keep them in?

But they didn't test his fences or his cattle guards,
Although they eyed him carefully each time he rode
His white horse onto Roundmound Hill to get a count
And fret anew about getting them into the yards

At Cassoday. I remember him pointing them out—
A cream-colored brindle muley, a yellowish steer
With long, tipped horns, and the red one, sharp horns
          never touched;
They grazed together all summer, each one watching out

For the others. Usually about eight of us gathered cattle
For Frank Klasser, but that fall there were a dozen
And more when it came time to ship the outlaw
Pasture, capable hands all, armed for battle

With rope and spur, though Klasser hated a rope—
And a rodeo cowboy. But Marshall and Kenneth Hoy
Were there, Peanuts Prewitt and the Youngs, Bus and Jim—
          calf ropers
And cow milkers in arena and pasture. If there was a hope

Of getting these cattle to the pens without a spill,
These men, along with Toad and Strut and Cliff,
Could do it, with us younger ones, Jay and Richard,
          Rita and Jim,
To follow the drag through the gates and up the hills

Through the flats, and into the cattle lanes that led
Past the lake the Santa Fe had built to water the thirsty
Steamers that pulled the stock cars from Aikman
          through Cassoday
And on to Matfield and Bazaar, the pens that fed

The grassfat steers to the Kansas City yards
By the thousands. The outlaws never took the lead
But stayed together, a length behind the light
Colored Brahma that led all the way, setting a hard

And steady pace past the Harsh Hill Pasture spring,
Where we got our last drink before the tea at Opal's
Cafe, then to Watkins, no other house along
The way, and that a mile off the trail that would bring

Us from the pastures to the lanes, the cattle strung
      out thin
Until we neared the tracks and the men in front
Slowed the leaders to bunch the herd for crossing
The rails—always touchy, for who knew when

A train might approach, causing the herd to spill
Back the way they had come. But we're lucky, no trains
Today; and, luckier still, the big outlaws
Follow the Brahma without pause or snort up the fill

And across the tracks, wing fence on our left, and through
The gate. By the time they pass through half a dozen
Openings and bounce off the back fence of the last pen
The drags are in the yards, the gate clapped to

Behind them. Klasser goes into the scale house with Jake,
Foreman for Welder-McCann, and the commission man,
Weaver, while we help draft off bunches of twenty
To push into the alleys, where the older hands will take

Them to be weighed, then back to the pens to await
The cattle loader. It's nearly two when we ride
To Opal's; ten hours since breakfast, roast beef and gravy
And corn, ice cream and pie to fill our plates.

But Frank barely touches his meal; he toys with his pie,
Not daring to breathe easy until the outlaws are on
The cars. Jake Jordan regales us with tales of Texas,
Of the pasture for horses, the little one, ten sections in size,

Behind the ranch house back home—but he knows it took
Only 3,000 acres of Kansas grass to fatten
These steers that had grown nothing but tall on 15,000
Acres in Texas. The train whistles in and we look

To our horses, loping back to the yards to take our places
For loading; the older hands stay on their mounts,
A nod to custom, and deference to their skill,
A badge of status they wear without a trace

Of arrogance. They cut out twenty-five
At a draft, pushing them down the alleyway;
The younger, stouter hands wrestle into place
The bullboards and wings before the steers arrive

To be crammed into the cars that in the spring
Had held half again that many. Our job was best,
We thought, to punch the steers on up the chute,
Reach over with a spur and rake the back of a straggling

Or reluctant steer. No stragglers as the first
Draft hits the chute, the Brahma lead steer coming
Up the ramp, the outlaw three still on
His tail. No need to hit them with a burst

Of yells or prods. And as they climb the ramp,
As alert as when they dodged a dozen Texas
Gathers, as calm as if still grazing Kansas
Grass, as purposeful as if approaching the damp

Bank of a stream for a drink, I feel a sense
Of sudden awe. Never again will cattle
Like these grace the Hills, these atavistic three—
Reminders of a time when plow and fence

Had yet to scar the plains. And I am there
To watch them scramble toward the railroad car
Laden with their mortality. They pass beneath
My outstretched hand; I reach bare palm to hair,

Touching each in turn, their backs firm
With fat, their coats coarse but smooth to the touch.
They neither flinch nor start, but ignore my hand
With regal aplomb, as if they had come to terms

With all there is to know of life. I see
Them disappear into the car, swallowed
Up into a general swirl of horns.
The door slides shut and is fastened, the wings swing free,

And the brakeman signals the next set of cars into place.
The outlaws are gone. And so now are most of the men
Who pushed the cattle down the alley that day,
Gone the way of steamers and stockyards, small trace

To mark the passing of an age. Yet even now
A whiff of creosote, or manure long dried, or pungent
Gourd brings to my mind as real as life
Itself, the day of horse, stockyard, and cow.

32.   *The Kansas City Stockyards*

(1985)

THE KANSAS CITY STOCKYARDS: once one of the great livestock trading centers of the world; shipping to and receiving from each of the 48 contiguous states; the largest livestock exchange building in the world (9 stories, 5 acres of floor space, 475 offices); facilities that covered 238 acres (including 175 paved, 87 under roof); 4,200 cattle pens, 700 hog pens, 450 sheep pens, 4 mule and horse barns; a total daily capacity of 175,000 head of livestock; a peak annual sales rate of 3 million head of cattle in 1918 (and that figure doesn't count calves, hogs, sheep, or horses).

The organization of the Kansas City Stockyards Company and the opening of the first livestock commission firm (Gilmore, Read and Company) occurred in 1871, but livestock trading had been conducted as early as 1862 in the general area where the yards were first built and now stand. The opening of the Abilene cattle pens on the Kansas Pacific in 1867 resulted in thirty-five thousand head of cattle being brought that year to Kansas City for feed, water, and rest, a number that doubled each of the next two years. The original yards, built in 1870, covered five acres and included eleven pens, fifteen unloading chutes, and a set of scales. Eight years later the yards had expanded across the state line into Missouri, covering nearly sixty acres, adding sheds for hogs and sheep, and boasting for the first time a real livestock exchange building—a three-story brick structure with commission offices, two banking rooms, a restaurant, a pool hall, a barber shop, and (for travel-begrimed drovers) a bath.

The Kansas City Stockyards have survived the economic disaster of the Great Depression and natural disasters including a ruinous fire in 1917 (which burned over half the yards and killed eleven thousand cattle and six thousand hogs) and two devastating floods, in 1903 and 1951 (both times flood waters reached into the second story of the exchange building but livestock losses were kept to a minimum). The Kansas

City yards have even outlasted archrival Chicago, at one time the largest livestock market in the world and the only one that was ever larger than Kansas City at its peak.

Today the exchange building still stands, home to the famed Golden Ox Restaurant and a few commission firms (struggling remnants of the scores that once operated), but most of the offices are empty save for the abandoned oak desks and file cabinets that once bulged with buy-and-sell orders.

Many, if not most, of the thousands and thousands of cattle shipped from the Cassoday stockyards went to Kansas City, and the stories that filtered back to my young ears were the stuff of fable—street cars and taxi cabs, hotels, saloons, burlesque houses, whiskey. Kansas may have been dry, but Missouri wasn't, and cattle owners or cowboys who took advantage of the Santa Fe's complimentary cattle passes rarely returned home without a bottle or two of snakebite medicine.

My firsthand acquaintance with Kansas City began in 1952, the year my grandfather died, the year we went with my other grandparents to visit Mother's uncles in Iowa, and the year that Dad fed out twenty-five or so two-year-old steers that he had not sold as stockers the year before. Usually we hauled our cattle to the community sale at El Dorado or to the Wichita stockyards, occasionally hiring Perry Whitham (who had a flatbed truck half again as big as our one-ton GMC) to help. But this particular year (I think my sister and I talked him into it) Dad decided to ship to Kansas City. We had just enough fat steers for one car, perhaps the smallest consignment ever to ship out of Cassoday, but it was a holiday for our whole family. I remember that Karl and Eunice Harsh went along (they may have sent cattle, too; I don't remember), we stayed at the Dixon Hotel (a favorite of ranchers), and I was allowed to buy a stockman's cane, just like the order buyers and commission men carried, as a souvenir.

I returned again to the Kansas City Stockyards on a May morning in 1985, wandering around the Livestock Exchange Building (many of its 475 offices now empty and the entire structure exuding an air of tiredness and resignation) until about 10:30 before heading over the auction-sales pavilion, built in 1970. The sale had been going on about half an hour. More than a 100, maybe 150 bidders were sitting on the bleacher seats semicircling the sale ring, auctioneer and clerk perched behind a counter well above the action. Three separate electric signs on the far wall recorded the number of cattle currently in the ring, the combined weight of the previous draft, and the average weight of the previous draft.

I sat for a while, trying to estimate the weight of the cattle as the auctioneer cried bids. I didn't do too well, which is one reason that I write and teach instead of raise cattle. After a dozen or so drafts had passed through, one of the men who had been working the ring took a seat beside me. He told me, in response to my questioning, that each commission firm was allowed to run fifty drafts through the ring before yielding to one of the other firms associated with the stockyards. On a good day, he said, each company will take several turns, but on a day like this one (around fifteen hundred head) some companies didn't have enough cattle to fill out even their first run. "How many companies are here?" I asked. "How big are the yards? How old is the exchange building?"

"See that man sitting over there?" he said. "The one in the front row with the straw hat? That's Dick Martin, a partner in Maxwell Furnish. You should talk to him. He's been here for seventy-seven years."

Dick Martin, I found out, is a walking history of the Kansas City Stockyards. I had thought, from the ring man's comment, that Martin was seventy-seven years old (a relatively young-looking seventy-seven), but in truth he was born in 1896. He had begun working in the exchange building as an office boy when he was only twelve, and ten years later he became a commission man for the Bowles Company. He has been buying and selling at Kansas City ever since.

Martin wouldn't hazard a guess when I asked about how many head of cattle went through Kansas City in its biggest year, but he did remember once in the late 1930s or early 1940s when sixty-four thousand head passed through in a single day. The yards were open seven days a week to receive cattle, with sales occurring Monday through Friday. He would often work from daylight through dark on Sunday just to get cattle—many of them the cattle we had sent up from Aikman, Cassoday, and Matfield Green earlier in the day—ready for the Monday market.

There were seventy-six commission firms operating simultaneously at one time, he told me; today there are ten, and, he thinks, soon some of them will have to merge. Among the current ten is H. Thies & Sons, which began its operations in Kansas City in 1885. John Clay (now Clay and Robison), is another of the old firms, as is Swift and Henry.

The packing plants are also gone; there were once six of them providing a steady market for the fat cattle that were sent to Kansas City. "We used to get those big Flint Hills grass-fat two- and three-year-old steers," he said, "and the packers made a lot of money on them." I had known that many of the cattle that we shipped off grass had gone to the Kansas City packers, but I didn't know until Martin told me that they would sometimes mix the carcasses and cuts of the Flint Hills steers with grain-fed beef from Iowa and Nebraska and sell it all for the same higher price. There was no government grading of beef back then, and the grass-fed beef was just as tasty and often as tender as the other.

The Kansas City Stockyards are surviving even without the packing plants, in Martin's opinion, because they have always been a good stocker and feeder market. They have a central location among the midwestern farm states and excellent transportation networks to the High Plains and the Southwest. Many Colorado feeder cattle still come into Kansas City, especially in the fall. Last year, according to Martin, eight hundred head were sent in a single shipment.

I asked about changes in cattle over the years. The Texas longhorns of the early days were largely gone by the time he began work in the yards, but most of the cattle were horned and showed a lot of Mexican influence. By the 1920s, however, livestock had been pretty well bred up: Herefords from

Colorado and the Southwest, Brahmas and British breeds from Texas.

Along with the upgrading of cattle herds came a decrease in Texas fever, a disease carried by ticks that thrived on the longhorn. When Martin first went to work in the yards, cattle were about evenly divided by a quarantine line—Texas and New Mexico cattle to the south side, others to the north. "When did this begin to change?" I asked. "Well," he pondered, "we got this new building in 1911, and it was shortly after that when we had a lot more cattle penned to the north. By the time the war was over, so was the quarantine."

The war, of course, was the First World War, and the "new building" the old Kansas City Livestock Exchange Building. (Largest in the world, remember? Nine stories, 5 acres of floor space, 475 offices—many of them now empty.) The Kansas City Stockyards, like Dick Martin, have endured by adapting. But for how much longer? Like a pioneer fighting off Indians, the Kansas City Stockyards are encircled by change and progress, dangerous foes to tradition anywhere. My sympathies are with tradition, especially one so closely linked to tallgrass cattle country.

Postscript

The Kansas City Stockyards have closed down for good. On September 26, 1991, the last cattle ever to be sold there passed through. There were only 150 head, probably the fewest ever handled in a single day. Back in the 1930s and 1940s a normal run was 30,000 head on Monday and 15,000 per day Tuesday through Friday. The biggest single-day total was 64,000 head back in October 1943. Ironically, the same month forty-eight years later saw the end of the Kansas City Stockyards; on October 5 they auctioned off the equipment and fixtures. Branding irons brought up to a hundred dollars, hog-watering buckets five dollars.

National Farms, perhaps the country's largest agricultural conglomerate, bought the exchange building, the facilities and pens, and the thirty-five remaining acres they sat on.

Most of the structures will be razed and the land used for office development. Current plans are to keep the sale barn and a few pens as a sort of theme park, a reminder of past glories.

You can't fight progress, they say. Well, you can, I guess, but it's damned hard to win.

33. *The Last Trail Herd from Texas*

WHEN WE were children, my sister Rita and I would often ride pastures with our father. Especially after a rain, when it was too wet to hay or cultivate, we'd saddle up and ride a few miles south to the Mosteller Pasture, where we summered much of our cow herd. Or maybe we'd go Over West, as Dad called the quarter in Section 8, where a smaller herd grazed. Or up north to the Knab or the Fluke. To pass the time we would get Dad to recite the long narrative poems he had learned in school—"The Ride of Jennie McNeal," "Charlotte, the Frozen Girl," "Sheridan's Ride"—or to tell us stories of his youth. We especially liked his dog stories (chiefly about greyhounds and coyote hunts) and horse stories (broncs he had ridden, trades he had made, and colts or mules he had raised and trained). One of our favorites, a visit to his uncle's ranch, had both dogs and horses in it and also chronicled what must have been one of the last trail drives from Texas to Kansas.

Dad was born in 1904 in northeastern Butler County near Cassoday, a cattle shipping center on the Santa Fe. The Hoys had moved from Ohio to the Flint Hills a few years after the Civil War, and some of the daughters had married and moved even farther west to homestead in western Kansas and eastern Colorado. One of these, my father's Aunt Etta, married Frank Goodnight of Englewood, Kansas.

I never met Uncle Frank, or if I did I don't remember it, being only three years old when he died, but from what I

Kenneth Hoy on Cap, c. 1937. (Author's collection.)

have been told he was the genuine article. He claimed a relationship, distant perhaps, to Charles Goodnight, the famous cowman of the Texas Panhandle, and occasionally bought stock, especially bison, from him. While his ranching operations pale when compared to those of his more famous relative, he was nevertheless quite an operator, running cattle on some thirty thousand acres of Clark County shortgrass. His teenage years were spent in the tallgrass of the southern Flint Hills near Dexter, however, where he escaped a gun battle but lost a finger to the Dalton Gang (see chapter 15).

Uncle Frank raised a few buffalo, some of which later were used to start the herd for which Garden City was renowned. Annabel Schnebly, one of Uncle Frank's nieces, remembers the delivery of some buffalo from the Texas ranch of Charles Goodnight: "I recall Uncle Frank saying his Uncle Charlie Goodnight was giving him ten buffalo, sent them by

truck from Texas to Englewood. Most everyone in Englewood was very excited about their arrival and gathered to see
the unloading of a bull and nine cows plus a baby calf born
on the way."

So to my dad, a nineteen-year-old boy who had never
been farther from home than his horse could travel after
cattle in a day, a visit to Uncle Frank's ranch in the High
Plains of southwestern Kansas was an exciting adventure.
Here is Dad's story, as I remember hearing it horseback on
those long, hot Kansas miles.

Uncle Jim Hoy's first wife died in 1923, and he was feeling
pretty low, so Dad [my grandfather, Frank Hoy] decided that
a visit to relatives might cheer him up. Uncle Frank had been
after us for a long time to bring our dogs out and hunt
coyotes with him, so we left Marshall to look after things (he
was still in high school anyway) and Uncle Jim, Dad, and I
drove to Englewood around the first of November.

We hauled out a few of our best greyhounds and our
saddles. Uncle Frank had plenty of horses and good dogs,
too. On the first hunt we jumped a coyote in a big pasture
and turned the dogs loose.

Our dogs from the tallgrass country were good enough at
dodging flint rocks and ducking under fences back home,
but when they hit their first patch of sandburs in the shortgrass prairie they just sat down and howled and yelped while
the native dogs chased the coyote down.

Of course, Uncle Frank and all my cousins thought it was
the funniest thing they had ever seen—each side had been
bragging up its dogs, and now ours were whining like pups.
Uncle Frank knew all the time what our dogs would do, but
he let us haul them all the way out to western Kansas anyway.

Even though our dogs weren't much good out there, we
did a lot of hunting, caught a lot of coyotes, and had a lot of
fun. In those days we didn't hunt out of pickups equipped
with two-way radios. We rode on horseback with the hounds,
and the coyote had a sporting chance.

I was always on the lookout for a good horse trade and

when my cousins told me about a nice little four-year-old brown Morgan I might be able to buy cheap, I was interested. The son of a druggist out in Englewood—I think his name was Roberts—wanted to be a cowboy and had bought this horse and done some riding for some local ranchers, but cowboying wasn't quite as much fun as he thought it was going to be, so he was ready to sell out. I bought his horse, or stole him, I thought, for $7.50, and that afternoon we went hunting again.

We had gone a long, long way without jumping any coyotes and must have been ten or twelve miles from Uncle Frank's ranch, or any other place as near as I could tell. That country all looked the same to me anyway, and my sense of direction wasn't too good on an overcast day.

Well, we jumped a coyote in a draw just beyond a wooden windmill, turned the dogs loose, and everybody took out over the hill after him. Except me. When I started to kick my new horse into a lope, he balked dead still and wouldn't move no matter what I did. I don't know if my cousins knew he was spoiled or not, but if they did the joke was on them because I soon unspoiled him.

I knew that if I didn't get him moving pretty quick, there would be no way I could keep up with the rest of them, and I sure didn't plan on getting lost out in the middle of all that buffalo grass.

There was a piece of split two-by-four lying by a windmill. I got off and got it and then got back on and spurred the horse. He didn't move, so I brought the board down between his ears—hard. He kind of shook and went to his knees and when he came up he took off. He was cured of that balking habit for as long as I had him, and I caught up with the others before they got out of sight.

After about ten days Dad and Uncle Jim were ready to go home, but my cousin Paul told me about a chance to drive some cattle for the neighboring Thies Ranch. They were bringing fifteen hundred head of three-year-old Hereford steers from Canadian, Texas, to Englewood to winter on wheat pasture. I think they had some land down there, or had leased a spread, and I guess it was cheaper to drive the steers up than to haul them. I was paid two or three dollars a day and my food, but I had to provide my own bedroll and three horses. I already had my saddle, slicker, chaps, and one horse. Paul outfitted me with the rest—some blankets and a tarp, his good old white horse, Gyp, for night-herding, and a good all-around cow horse named Buck.

Buck was the horse they used for cutting. Paul said he was so good you could cut chickens or pigs on him. I didn't have to do any sorting on the drive, but he was a good cow horse and my little Morgan got any other bad habits he might have had worked out of him by the time we got back.

I don't remember the names of all the people on the drive. There were about eleven men plus a cook and a wrangler. The cook was named Stoval or Stowall and he drove a chuck wagon pulled by one team of horses. Then there was a young rancher named Ralph Cole. He lived at Englewood and I remember he had a wife and kid and there were a couple of goats around his place.

The foreman of the Thies Ranch was the trail boss. His name was Lon Ford and he was pretty colorful. He wore a gun, a Colt sidearm, and some of the other fellows on the drive told me he had had killed two or three men with it in his time. He was about forty and although, according to some on the drive, he had been in prison for cattle theft, he was later made sheriff of Clark County. Ford told me he had to be careful his feet didn't freeze because he had no feeling in them and couldn't tell when they were getting cold. When he was younger his feet had stunk pretty bad, so he rubbed them with some sort of patent medicine that took away not only the stink but the feeling, too.

When we got ready to leave for Kansas, Ford had one of the cowboys rope a steer and he shot him with his six-gun and the cook butchered him on the spot. Beans and that fresh beef made into mulligan stew fed us on the drive. For breakfast we had bacon, biscuits cooked in a dutch oven, fried potatoes, and strong black coffee. We drank mostly from water barrels tied to the sides of the chuck wagon, though the weather was so cold we didn't get too thirsty.

I remember going through one mile of fenced lane, either at the beginning or end of the drive; otherwise, we drove across grass all the way. We didn't have any storms, meet with any farmers or Indians, come near any towns, have any stampedes, or have any kind of unusual trouble at all. Occasionally we could see a farmstead and we crossed several trails, but we didn't run into any other people on the whole drive. Crossing the Cimarron could have been trouble because of the quicksand, but Ford knew where to cross and we didn't get into any kind of a bind.

I was used to long drives anyway because cattle coming into summer pasture at Cassoday were unloaded at DeGraff and driven fifteen to thirty miles east to the Hills. But we didn't have to night-herd cattle back home and this was a new experience. Ford told us at the start that when we were riding night-herd we were supposed to sing or hum because the sound of our voice would let the cattle know where we were and keep them calm.

We bedded the herd down every night about an hour or so before dark. From then until we left, shortly after dawn the next day, there were always two men watching the cattle. Everybody rode night-herd every night, each of us taking a two-hour turn. We would circle the herd, humming or singing, and when we met, we would turn around and ride another half-circle till we met again. The cattle were never corralled while we were on the trail. During the day I would usually ride the right or left rear flank.

The drive took seven days. When we got back, the day before Thanksgiving, we made it into town as quick as we could for a trip to the barbershop. We hadn't had a chance to shave, and not many chances to wash, on the whole drive.

I left for home the day after Thanksgiving, riding my new Morgan, who was a whole lot easier to get along with than when I had first bought him. I had a little over two hundred miles to go and I made it in five days, riding in good but cold weather through four or five inches of snow that fell on Thanksgiving Day.

I went through Ashland, Coldwater, Pratt, Kingman, Wichita, and El Dorado, staying all night at farmhouses along the way. Nobody refused to let me stay and they all fed me and my horse for nothing, even though I offered to pay.

By the time Dad hit the end of his travel narrative, we were usually getting pretty close to home. No more stories until the next time to ride pastures. As I look back, I realize how lucky he was to experience what had to have been one of the last trail drives through open country with a big herd of cattle, a chuck wagon, and an Old West, gun-carrying foreman. He might well be the last man alive to have driven cattle from Texas to Kansas.

Part Six

PLAY

ACCORDING TO Guy Logsdon, no other occupational group in the country has composed as many poems and songs as have cowboys. Guy should know. Not only does he have a bulging file of cowboy songs, including the risqué ones, but in 1989 he published many of them in the latest of what has been a steady stream of cowboy-verse collections that goes back to 1908. That was the year that Jack Thorp, a working cowboy, published *Songs of the Cowboys,* which was followed two years later by *Cowboy Songs and Other Frontier Ballads,* the first major work of the greatest of American folk song collectors, John Lomax. Between then and now came a large number of popular (and bowdlerized) collections, then a spate of serious collections in the 1970s and early 1980s by academics Alta and Austin Fife and Jim Bob Tinsley, radio singer John White, and rodeo cowboy Glenn Orhlin.

At first you might wonder, given the many different occupations in this country that have produced folk songs—mining, for instance, or logging, or farming, riverboating, soldiering, railroading, even working on a chain gang—just why did working with cattle and horses generate the largest poetic output? Part of the answer is subject matter, the dangerous and exciting aspects of the job itself. Not that the other jobs didn't have their dangers and disasters, but a cowboy, particularly a nineteenth- or early twentieth-century cowboy, literally took his life in his hands every morning when he took the buck out of his mustang-blooded horse, or any time during the day when he shook out a loop and fastened it onto a longhorn that often was bigger than the horse he was riding.

And then there were outlaws and Indians to fight, stampedes to quell, flooded rivers to cross, rattlesnakes and lightning bolts to dodge. Not to mention the quirks and foibles of his daily contact with cows, horses, dogs, ranch owners, and other cowboys. Or the splendors of nature that constantly

surrounded him—if he wasn't eating too much dust while
riding drag on a trail herd to notice. No question about it,
the old-time cowboy had plenty to write about, and so does
his modern counterpart, even though many of the early-day
mortal dangers, such as outlaws and stampedes, have since
given way to governmental bureaucrats and animal-rights ac-
tivists that threaten not individual cowboys, but the very
occupation.

But one advantage the cowboy poet had over the rail-
roader poet or the logger poet or the miner poet was that he
had plenty of leisure time, and plenty of breath, to sing his
songs or to recite his poetry. Not that the cowboy wasn't
working from before sun-up until after sunset every day for
week after week, but the dangerous, exciting part of his job,
the part that gave him plenty of material to write about,
actually took up only a small fraction of his time—say 20
percent at most.

The biggest danger in the remaining 80 percent of the job
was being bored to death. Living solitary for weeks on end at
a lonely line camp. Trailing cattle day after day from Texas to
Kansas, or on to Montana, plodding along with excruciating
slowness over the dusty, featureless plains. Riding night-herd
when he was so bone weary that the only way he could stay
awake and keep from falling off his horse was to talk to
himself or sing. What else was there to do but make up verse?

Railroad or lumberjack or chain-gang songs must have
been composed and sung in the morning. Somehow I just
can't imagine John Henry or Leadbelly having enough energy,
or breath, to be singing at sunset after swinging that nine-
pound hammer all day long. But the cowboy? His horse was
doing all of the hard work anyway, so why shouldn't he sing?

And sing he did, around the campfire, at the bunkhouse,
while on the trail or riding night-herd. John Lomax tells of
singing contests held on west Texas ranches during the late
nineteenth century, singdowns where the best singers from
all the ranches in a given area would come together for a
kind of singing endurance contest that might go on all night
and into the next morning. One cowboy would start out

singing a song, then the next one in the circle would have to
sing a different one, and so on around the ring until a cowboy had exhausted his repertoire, or his memory. Then he
would drop out, but the contest would keep going, like an
old-fashioned spelling bee, until only one cowboy was left
standing—and singing.

Today much of the cowboy lifestyle has been co-opted by
American culture in general. People from all walks of life,
from truck drivers to attorneys and accountants, and from all
parts of the country, but especially the West, wear boots and
jeans and big hats, even if they have never been on a horse in
their life. Movies and popular fiction have transformed the
working cowboy into an American icon, while rodeo cowboys
have transformed the skills of ranch work into sporting contests with but scant relationship to life on the range. Until
recently only the poems and songs, some from the nineteenth century and some from the early twentieth, seemed to
have escaped the glare of the spotlight and were still being
recited and sung on ranches throughout the West much as
they had been a century earlier.

But all that changed in late January 1985 when folklorist
Hal Cannon of Utah helped to produce the first Cowboy
Poetry Gathering out in Elko, Nevada. Cowboy verse suddenly became big news, while cowboy versifiers, such as Baxter Black, Wallace McRae, and Waddy Mitchell, began pop-
ping up everywhere from public television to the Tonight
Show. Since then Elko has become a kind of National Finals
of a burgeoning movement of cowboy poetry gatherings that
have sprung up throughout the west—big ones at the National Cowboy Hall of Fame in Oklahoma, at the National
Cowboy Symposium in Texas, at the annual Cowboy's Christmas in Arizona, at the Pike's Peak Gathering in Colorado
Springs, and at dozens of smaller ones at fairs, rodeos, and
other occasions that lend themselves to what some cowboy
poets themselves have called "dogie doggerel."

One result of all this activity has been the development of
a circuit of semiprofessional cowboy poets, with the further
result that cowboy poetry has begun to lose the spontaneity

of its folk origins. But not entirely. In the fall of 1990 we held the first all-Kansas cowboy and cowgirl poetry gathering in Strong City (the heart of the Flint Hills) and the folk tradition was palpable, from the largely rural audience to the dozen performers. None of them were "names," just cowboys, cowgirls, ranchers, veterinarians, team ropers, and horse breakers (only one from outside the Flint Hills region) who happened also to write poems about what they do.

The performance opened and closed with silver-screen cowboy songs harmonized by a band called Bluestem, a fitting name for a gathering here in the tallgrass. The poems ranged from the humorous (cattle roundups and misbehaving cowdogs) to the pensive (mustangs, night fishing, and loading cattle onto railroad stockcars) to the nostalgic (old cow horses) to the philosophical (ropers who tie hard and fast). The evening was dedicated to the memory of Lou Hart, a working cowboy on the Crocker Ranch who, sometime between 1906 and 1910, wrote a poem called "Springtime at Crockers" that depicts with accuracy and feeling the daily life of a Flint Hills cowboy at the turn of the century.

What made the evening a success was authenticity, real people responding to their genuine feelings for working with livestock and living with the land—and putting those feelings into verse. If the bond that emerged that night between performer and audience is an accurate indication, then cowboy poetry is alive and well in the Flint Hills—as it is throughout the rest of the West.

In fact, if numbers are an indication, cowboy poetry is robust. Not only did old-time cowboys write more songs and poems than any other folk group in the country, but contemporary cowboy poets are literally flooding the market with paperback booklets and cassette tapes of their works. When Hal Cannon prepared his 1985 anthology, *Cowboy Poetry: A Gathering,* he found and consulted over two hundred collections of poetry, most of it privately published, and over ten thousand individual poems. I don't know how many printings Cannon's anthology has been through, but the last I heard it had sold nearly fifty thousand copies. That must make it, except for textbooks, the best-selling poetry anthology ever. Or damn close to it.

But is it poetry? Well, some is and some isn't. Much cowboy poetry is nothing more than stories (or jokes) in verse. There is no question that much cowboy poetry is mere doggerel. There is little innovation in form: the ballad stanza abounds. Cowboys might be able to count cattle, but most of them darn sure can't count syllables. And many will butcher the syntax or stretch credulity to get a rhyme—or even get within shouting distance of it. One finds here pure nostalgia, sentimental religiosity, and mindless patriotism as well as brutality, sexism, and occasional racism (especially in the earlier stuff). Is it poetry? Not all that much of it is.

But on the other hand, if you would bring together a bunch of MFAs (Masters of Fine Arts—the usual degree held by academic poets) from university creative writing programs around the country and take a look at their collected works, how much real poetry would you find? Not all that much. About the same percentage, I figure, as you would find among the cowboys. And if both groups were to perform their poems aloud, there's no doubt in my mind which group would draw—and keep—the larger crowd. Yes, much cowboy poetry is trite and predictable, but much more of it is excellent story-in-verse, and some even has those elements of universality that are the hallmark of greatness.

My point is that real poetry is a rare commodity, rare in any age or among any group, even professional poets. Good story telling is less rare, but still not common, and the saving grace of the less poetic of the cowboy poets is that they are good storytellers. Moreover, cowboy poetry performs an important cultural function in documenting a way of life. It is "memory" poetry in the same way that some folk artists are "memory" painters—it preserves traditions and a sometimes vanishing lifestyle. And it is not without contemporary relevance in its reflection of impatience with bureaucracy and with its antagonism to many of the irritations of the modern world. And if many cowboy poets use standard metrical and rhyme schemes (thereby following tradition), there are others who are innovative enough to write some excellent free verse.

In May of 1991 Dana Gioia, a poet outside the pale of academe (he's a business executive), published in the *Atlantic* a lengthy, reasoned, and provocative essay, "Can Poetry Matter?" His thesis is that the relevancy of poetry has been constricted by the bonds of MFA programs, that contemporary poetry has no apparent readership or appeal beyond the network of little magazines and incestuous (you-invite-me-and-I'll-invite-you) university readings. At the end of his essay Gioia makes six suggestions for reinvigorating poetry, to make it again "part of American public culture." Here is his list: (1) poets should recite the work of other poets, not just their own, at public readings; (2) readings should occur in conjunction with exhibits or performances of other arts; (3) poets should write candid criticism of poetry, using real language, not academic jargon; (4) anthologies should include only poems genuinely admired by the editor, not the work of his or her friends; (5) poetry teachers should spend less time on analysis and more on performance and memorization; and (6) poets should use radio to expand poetry's audience.

Dana Gioia should come to Elko or Lubbock or Colorado Springs sometime. He'd see that cowboy poets are already doing most of what he has suggested. (1) I have yet to attend a cowboy poetry gathering where performers did not recite poems by others, particularly the classic authors, such as Badger Clark, Bruce Kiskaddon, Gail Gardner, or Curley Fletcher; (2) gatherings almost invariably include music as well as poetry and many times there are accompanying exhibits of western art and sculpture as well as displays of the more functional trappings of ranching: boots, saddles, spurs, hats, rawhide and horsehair weaving; (3) you can't really expect cowboys to write poetry criticism, but they damn sure have their opinions about what is good and what isn't and they are not averse to giving those opinions in straightforward language; (4) I suppose that cowboys are no more immune from back scratching than any other group of artisans; (5) perfor-

mance (usually memorized) is the hallmark of cowboy poetry; and (6) cowboy poets, among them Baxter Black,
Waddy Mitchell, Wally McRae, Paul Zarzyski, and Ian Tyson,
have been effectively using the airwaves (the "Tonight Show,"
Larry King, National Public Radio, and TNN, among other
venues) for several years.

Is cowboy poetry real poetry? Well, it sure seems to measure up to Gioia's standards. And it seems to me to meet an
even more famous standard: William Wordsworth once defined poetry as "emotion recollected in tranquillity written
in the real language of men." Hell, that's what cowboys have
been doing ever since the days of the Old Chisholm Trail.
Curley Fletcher sure didn't write "The Strawberry Roan"
while he was trying to make the ride. And if you have any
doubts about the realness of the language, just read the version of that poem that Guy Logsdon includes in *The Whore-
house Bells Were Ringing, and Other Songs Cowboys Sing.*

35. *The National Cowboy Symposium and Celebration*

(June 1989)

MY JOB in academe often requires that I attend meetings of
one sort or another, often the sort I would just as soon
avoid. I'm sure that many in the business world, or in government, or the health professions—you name it—share my
aversion. But a couple of weeks ago I had a chance to participate in the most satisfying and useful meeting I have ever
attended, the first National Cowboy Symposium and Celebration. The last word in the title set the tone for the whole
meeting—it was a genuine celebration of the culture of the
American cowboy.

Imagine a group of old-time and contemporary ranchers
and cowboys trading stories; then throw in an academic conference, an art exhibit, a book fair, a music festival, a writers'
convention, a living-history museum, and a poetry reading,
all these events with the cowboy as a theme; finally add a

team roping, a cutting-horse contest, and a barbecue and you'll have some idea of what went on down in Lubbock on the first weekend of June. So much was happening that I couldn't take in everything, but what I did see and hear was well worth the three-hour delay in the Dallas airport.

I met a number of good writers, including Elmer Kelton and John Erickson. I got to hear Don Edwards, Red Steagall, Waddie Mitchell, and other cowboy singers and poets perform. I heard Paul Stone, cowboy singer and Yale doctoral student, sing a song about Tom Blasingame (see chapter 7). I got to lean up against an arena gate with Jim Shoulders, sixteen-time world champion rodeo cowboy, and listen to the story of his experience (not positive, thanks to the market collapse of the early 1970s) in pasturing steers in tallgrass country near my home town. He and I came out even in the team roping; we both missed.

Authenticity pervaded. There were movie makers there, but thanks to *Lonesome Dove*, they were more concerned with accuracy than with mythology. Even country singer Red Steagall and actor Barry Corbin (the deputy in *Lonesome Dove* and the astronaut on "Northern Exposure"), both with roots in the Lubbock area, were cowboys before they were entertainers.

Among the many spur-, hat-, and bootmakers exhibiting was Jay Griffith, who made a pair of boots for me when he was operating the Blucher Company a few years back. Jay's origins go deep into cow country, and in our visit he told a story that epitomized for me the pervasive tone of authenticity at the National Cowboy Symposium.

Griffith's grandfather, shortly after the Civil War, worked on a Texas ranch, but neither he nor his fellow riders had much money. Their saddles were patched together and they wore laced-up brogan shoes and held their pants up with a single piece of yarn passed diagonally from front to back over one shoulder. One day a newcomer joined the crew, a man who had been north with the herds and had come back with new boots and a big hat. He ridiculed the "shoestring and yarn-gallus cowboys," as he called them, until the night that six thousand steers penned in a stone corral near Hamilton,

Texas, broke the gate loose and stampeded. The drovers finally got the herd slowed and turned, but when daylight came they saw the new hand trapped on his horse in the middle of the milling cattle, calling for help to get past the still-lively longhorns. "The hell with you," was the response. "You've got all those fancy clothes and equipment—get yourself out."

Experience, not just the outfit, makes the cowboy. And experience abounded at Lubbock, amidst a variety of outfits, from Great Basin buckaroo to south Texas vaquero. Congratulations to Alvin Davis of the Ranching Heritage Center at Texas Tech University for coming up with the idea, and to the many people who helped him in putting on a whale of a gathering.

Postscript

I have attended each National Cowboy Symposium and Celebration, the latest one during the second week of September 1994, and they keep getting bigger and better. It continues to be a whale of a gathering.

36. *The Chadron-to-Chicago Horse Race*

SEVERAL years ago, back when they were still making lots of Westerns, I saw "Bite the Bullet," a film about a long-distance horse race. I don't recall the exact destination of the race, or the precise distance, but it was in the hundreds of miles. I do recall Gene Hackman and Jan-Michael Vincent and Candace Bergen (long before she was Murphy Brown) riding their horses so mercilessly that they wouldn't have gotten five miles if the race had been run over real geography instead of the Hollywood variety.

One thing accurate about the movie, though, was its central action: endurance races were not uncommon on the Great Plains in the waning days of the open range. One of the most famous, and longest, occurred in 1893, the year that

Frederick Jackson Turner declared the frontier closed. Billed as a thousand-mile cowboy race, the course was probably nearer nine hundred miles, running from Chadron, Nebraska, through Iowa and ending at the arena of the Buffalo Bill Wild West Show at the Columbian Exposition in Chicago.

Promoters expected as many as twenty-five to thirty cowboys to vie for the thousand dollars–plus in prize money; humane-society types from the East were worried that as many as three hundred would show up. Rules stipulated that riders could use two horses "bred and raised west of the Mississippi" and that the combined weight of rider and gear could not be less than 150 pounds. Entrants had to register at thirteen checkpoints along the way, where their health, and that of their mounts (road-branded with a "2" under the mane), could be checked. The purpose of the race was to demonstrate the prowess of western horses and horsemen and at the same time symbolically represent the conquest of the American West.

The race began at 5:30 P.M. on June 13, with but nine entrants (owners, where different from riders, are listed in parentheses): Doc Middleton, Dave Douglas (Mike Elmore), Emmet Albright (P. G. Cooper), and Joe Gillespie from Nebraska; George Jones (Abe Jones), John Berry (Jack Hale), and Charles Smith from South Dakota; James "Rattlesnake Pete" Stephens from Kansas; and Joe Campbell from Colorado. Only Campbell limited himself to one horse.

Stephens, Gillespie, and Middleton set the pace during the first half of the race, but John Berry took over the lead at Waterloo, Iowa, and went on to win. At 9:30 on the morning of June 27 he pulled into Chicago—after thirteen days and sixteen hours on the road—having ridden the last 150 miles in only twenty-four hours. He left his bay gelding, Sandy, at DeKalb and finished the race on Poison, a sorrel stallion. Berry, however, was riding under protest, his sponsor having helped to lay out the route of the race. The second place finisher, Emmet Albright, was also disqualified when officials learned that he had shipped himself and his two horses by train from Dixon, Illinois, to Chicago for the last lap.

Joe Gillespie was declared the official winner, although the riders voted Berry a healthy share of the pot. In fact, all riders, except Dave Douglas, who had dropped out early, shared in the prize money. The real winners, however, were the horses, who arrived in better shape than their riders and were celebrated thus by Buffalo Bill: "This race showed the world . . . the hardiness of the bronco . . . cowboys know that the horse is their best friend and that its best endeavors can be brought out by kindness and care." Someone should have told that to Hackman, Bergen, et al.

37. *Ranch Rodeos*

SEVERAL times during the past few years I've had the honor of being one of the judges for the all-around cowboy and horse contests at the Kansas Championship Ranch Rodeo at Medicine Lodge. One of the advantages of the job is getting to see some fine cow horses in action and getting to watch up close some of the best working cowboys to be found anywhere, men such as Rod Breech, Wayne Bailey, Burkie Adcock, Rex Bugbee, and Rick Hinkle. All but the last-named, by the way (who cowboys for the Tate Ranch out in Kearney County), are products of the tallgrass. Rod, Wayne, and Rex grew up in the Flint Hills of Greenwood, Chase, and Lyon counties, respectively, while Burkie is a native of the Osage who moved up to a Kansas ranch several years ago.

Another advantage is that it has gotten me to thinking about the nature of rodeo cowboys and ranch cowboys. At one time all rodeo cowboys were ranch cowboys, even though not all ranch cowboys had rodeoed. That was back in the trail driving days that followed the Civil War, a time when working cowboys would get together to match skills in bronc riding or steer roping—working skills they used every day at the roundup or on the trail. From these matches grew exhibitions and contests that evolved into modern rodeo—a bronc riding at Deer Trail, Colorado, in 1869; a steer roping at Pecos,

Texas, in 1883, and another one the following year at Dodge City; a combination of roping and riding events at Prescott, Arizona, in 1888; and many more in other parts of the West.

Many of the early-day professional rodeos, such as the Cattlemen's Carnival at Garden City, Kansas (which began in 1904), had fifteen or more contest events, including chuck wagon races, calf branding, relay races, and wild-cow milking. But by the 1920s, as rodeo was becoming more and more a professional sport rather than an aspect of cowboy folklife, the contests began to be limited to a half-dozen or so standard events: bareback-bronc riding, calf roping, saddle-bronc riding, steer wrestling, bull riding, and occasionally team roping and single-steer roping.

At the same time that rodeo events were losing their resemblance to real ranch work, the competing cowboys were getting farther and farther from their ranch roots. So much so, in fact, that today many top rodeo cowboys, including world champions, have never worked on ranches. After all, if you are growing up in a big city, it's hard to learn ranching skills, but you can learn rodeo skills simply by going to a bull-riding or calf-roping school. As old-time rodeo producer Wilber Countryman from my home town says about rodeo cowboys, "In the old days, a cowboy was just a cowboy, but nowadays he's an athlete on a race horse."

By the 1970s rodeo cowboys were, except for their attire, nearly indistinguishable from other professional athletes. But then a funny thing happened in range country, where rodeo was born. As professional rodeo got slicker and slicker, the prize-money purses larger and larger, the contestants faster and better, ranch cowboys decided to take back their sport. They began to hold ranch rodeos, or range contests as they are sometimes called, featuring events that are closely related to real ranch work, with contestants who earn their livings by working on ranches, riding horses that are used out in the pastures and in the sorting pens. In other words, rodeo has returned to its roots.

As far as I've been able to determine, the first modern-day ranch rodeo was held at Wichita Falls, Texas, in 1980. (See

Wilber Countryman (*left*) and Kenneth Hoy getting ready to take a string of relay-race horses from Cassoday to the rodeo at El Dorado, 1927. (Author's collection.)

Behind the chutes at the first Countryman Rodeo, 1938. *Left to right:* Jay B. Parsons, Don Sturgeon, Marshall Hoy, Kenneth Hoy, Wilber Countryman, Beanie Hoyt. (Author's collection.)

Ranch Rodeos in West Texas, by Lawrence and Sonia Clayton, for descriptions of events and photographs of contests and contestants at Texas ranch rodeos.) By mid-decade the movement had begun to gather steam, with contests in Albany, Breckenridge, and Abilene, as well as some in Oklahoma and Kansas. Oklahoma held its first statewide ranch rodeo championships in 1985, and although the cowboys and contests were authentic, the setting, Guthrie's magnificent indoor Lazy E Arena, was not exactly true to range conditions. I attended the 1987 Oklahoma contest, taking along my son, then sixteen years old, and my father and uncle, eighty-three and eighty respectively. Dad and Uncle Marshall, in assessing the abilities displayed in the various contests, were their usual discerning (that is to say, scornfully critical) selves. They liked the roping and the roping horses, but thought that the Oklahoma bronc riders left something to be desired. But then, between pasture rodeos and horse breaking, these two had probably been on a thousand bucking horses since they first started riding in about 1910. And they figured out a better way to cut cattle out for team penning long before the final team that night did it, successfully (by sending an extra rider into the herd), their way. It was fun for me, and instructive for Josh, to see the contemporary working cowboys competing and at the same time to hear commentary from the perspective of a century and a half of combined pasture-wisdom.

By 1989 there were so many ranch rodeos being held in Kansas that some folks from Medicine Lodge decided to hold the first state championship in the Sunflower State. Unlike the Oklahoma championship, the setting at Medicine Lodge was not in an indoor arena, but outdoors in the rugged Gypsum Hills, near the natural amphitheater where the triennial Peace Treaty Pageant is held. Teams came from ranches across the state—the Flint Hills, the Smoky Hills, the Gypsum Hills, the High Plains—but it was the Tate Ranch from western Kansas that rode away with the first-place trophy in each of the first two years of competition. The hometown Chain Ranch won in 1991.

Events will vary from ranch rodeo to ranch rodeo. Some events are ones you would find in a regular rodeo—team roping, for instance, or saddle-bronc riding—but with rule changes that make them more like real life. Bronc riders, for instance, must use a stock saddle, not a regulation contest saddle, and, although they ride for eight seconds, they are allowed to hold on with both hands. Or, if they are good enough, to fan the bucking horse with a quirt or a hat in their free hand.

Some ranch-rodeo events, such as the wild-horse race, wild-cow milking, and calf branding, were standard at early-day rodeos. Some, such as team penning and cutting-horse contests, have been developed over the years as free-standing competitions. Still others, such as cattle doctoring, double mugging (roping a yearling from a horse, then wrestling it to the ground by hand and tying it), trailer loading, and the feed-sack race, have been especially developed for ranch rodeos.

Besides the ranch rodeos, which usually have half a dozen or so events, contemporary cowboys have also held single-event contests. I went to a bull-cutting at Cassoday in the early 1980s, modeled on one that had been held at Salina the year before, which in turn was modeled on one held in Texas. The tallgrass contests featured three-person teams heading, heeling, and castrating yearling bulls in quarter-section pastures, whereas the Lone Star contest, in true bigger-is-better Texas fashion, sent teams out into a twelve-thousand-acre pasture to look for their animals (each one was numbered and teams drew numbers). Bull-cutting contests seem relatively rare, but pasture-roping contests are fairly common (see chapter 39). Pasturemen in the Flint Hills, where pasturing transient summer cattle is the norm, have devised a contest based on the kind of preparation incoming cattle normally receive. Three-person teams compete in an annual going-to-grass chute-working contest held near Paxico. Each team vaccinates, implants, and ear tags three head of yearling stock; they are judged on both time and technique.

Because ranch rodeos are an outgrowth of ranching culture, they are often accompanied by other reflections of that culture. Cowboy singers and poets, for instance, will often perform at a ranch rodeo, and many times a cowboy dance will provide a fitting, and fun, conclusion to the festivities. Saddlemakers, spurmakers, and other artisans often display their work in conjunction with a ranch rodeo, while some shows have contest events for such traditional crafts as chuck-wagon cooking, knot tying, and rawhide braiding. Many also have displays of western paintings and sculptures, such as the exhibit that Earl Kuhn arranges for the Medicine Lodge show.

A major reason for the popularity of ranch rodeos is that rural people can relate to the events. After all, they themselves have calves to brand—or must occasionally load a cantankerous critter into a trailer or manage to stay with a pitching horse. Moreover, they are watching their neighbors compete in these action-packed events—the teenage boy from just down the road, the woman from the ranch across the river, the seventy-year-old hired hand who remembers the days of railroad shipping.

At the same time urban dwellers can see an exciting horseback competition that will educate them about how things are really done on the range. In the swirl and hubbub of contemporary life, ranch rodeo provides a simultaneous glimpse into the past and the present of the real life of the working cowhand.

38. *Goat Ropers*

REMEMBER the bumper sticker popular a few years back— "Goat Ropers Need Love Too"? To tell the truth, I couldn't figure out the humor in that slogan until someone explained to me what a goat roper was: a would-be cowboy who wore a feed-store cap, drove a twelve-year-old rusted-out pickup truck, lived in a mobile home on a six-acre plot on the outskirts of town, and kept a skinny horse in a little pen out behind the rabbit hutches. The have-nots, in other words, were twitting the fancy-horse crowd. It takes serious money to follow the horse-show circuit and manifest ability to rodeo successfully, but not much of either commodity to chase goats around the backyard. Or maybe the haves were rubbing salt into the wounds of the have-nots—irony sometimes meanders around in strange ways.

At any rate, the reason I initially missed the humor in this bumper sticker was that I had never thought of goat roping as a second-class pursuit. After all, my friends and I used to rope goats in our earlier years—goats are cheaper than Brahma calves for the beginning roper and much less likely to be injured. Or to injure a thirteen-year-old kid with a pigging string in his teeth. In fact, if you can rope one of these ducking, dodging, snake-necked creatures running wide open, you can rope about anything. Many good ropers have honed their skills on goats.

I remember, for instance, as a boy watching Peanuts Prewitt rope goats on Wilber Countryman's ranch a few miles south of Cassoday. Wilber loved to see people rope and Peanuts loved to rope. Wilber would load four or five goats onto the back of his pickup, then drive out to a nice, level spot in the middle of the section pasture where he lived. There he would unload one goat and someone to hold it while he drove on about a hundred yards. Once released, the goat took off like a streak for his fellows, the roper in hot pursuit. If caught and tied, the goat, when turned loose, would usually trot on up to the pickup and hop in, but if the roper missed, the goat would literally sail through the air in leaping onto the pickup bed at full speed.

Wilber himself used to rope goats with my Uncle Marshall back in the 1930s, following a practice established in the Flint Hills a couple of decades earlier by Gwyn Liggett of Rosalia. Liggett, one of the top ropers of his day in this area, held weekly goat ropings on his ranch, and people came from miles away, both to rope and to watch. Rodeo cowboys of wider renown, such as J. Ellison Carroll and Clay McGonigall, were also avid goat ropers. At least they became so after

Texas, among other states, outlawed the contest roping of calves and steers. The wealthy livestock owners who pushed for the adoption of these antiroping laws apparently didn't consider goats worthy of protection.

I remember once hearing a story about some goat roping Bob Crosby and Ike Rude undertook a half century or so ago, one of those stories that should have happened even if it didn't. These two roping greats were between rodeos and killing a little time somewhere on the High Plains, maybe Rude's ranch in western Oklahoma. Anyway one morning they decided to rope some goats for practice—one man was to turn goats loose for the other until the roper missed, then they would switch jobs. Crosby won the toss of the coin and began to rope, catching something like forty or fifty goats before he missed. Then Rude mounted up and started roping. All the rest of the morning he roped. All that afternoon he roped. All the next morning he roped—until Crosby finally said the hell with it and quit.

So don't feel bad if someone calls you a goat roper. He may mean it as an insult, but you could find yourself in much worse company.

39. *Pasture-Roping Contest*

As NOTED earlier, pasture roping generally differs greatly from contest roping, but in the past few years there has been a move to merge the two, evidence of the cowboy's natural inclination to make play of his work. The first pasture-roping contest I knew of was held during the summer of 1987, staged by Walt Stotler, who has a team-roping arena a few miles east of our place south of Emporia. Walt got the idea from a contest he had seen near Vernon, Texas.

The rules were relatively simple: two ropers to a team, an eighty-foot head start for the steer, get a rope on him, remove a sale-barn tag from his back, and ride back across the finish line with both ropes and the tag. The arena was on the south side of the pasture, next to a gravel road, and the steers were started from a catch pen on the far end, headed out into the pasture. You could take as many loops as necessary within the four-minute time limit, but running a steer through the fence was a disqualification. Roping conditions were, to put it mildly, authentic—temperature over one-hundred degrees, wind gusting to twenty-five miles per hour, cattle (the previous year's corriente roping steers) big, fresh, and lively. The pasture was a quarter section of native grass, relatively smooth at the starting point but with draws, ponds, rocks, brush, and an occasional hedge tree to contend with if the chase went beyond the first two loops. Contestants came from as far away as St. Joseph, Missouri, although most were from the Emporia area or the three or four counties adjoining.

The thrills started early. The first ropers (out of twenty-seven teams entered, including my son and me) chased their steer out into the pasture, then back around to the east side of the arena, where they ran into the harrow used to smooth the arena and got tangled up with a creep feeder. One rider on the next team raced across the finish line and ran his horse into the guy wire of an electric pole, horse and rider both narrowly escaping serious injury. The third team could have won it all—the first rider caught the steer quickly, but his partner's horse bucked every time it was kicked into a lope. Another team also first-looped its steer close in, but as the roper was racing across the finish line, his mugger was still standing back where they had turned the steer loose, looking in vain for the sale tag he had lost in the tallgrass. A couple of good runs were ruined when horses got away from muggers and had to be chased down. One exasperated (and winded) cowboy, once he had finally caught his mount, had this terse response to a ribbing about needing to train his horse better: "I got a gun in the truck."

Only one team failed to catch its steer (they quit after two loops, knowing they were not going to win), although four or five ran past the time limit. My son and I finished in the top third with a minute-and-a-half run (I missed my first throw, but Josh caught with his), but we were well out of the money.

The winning time was 34.97 seconds, only .02 of a second faster than the runners-up.

One member of the third-place team, Jim Burum, who has worked on the Braum Ranch near Emporia for the past several years, afterwards told me of some of the pasture-roping contests he had participated in near his native Pampa, Texas. The cattle, he said, were a little wilder and teams were required to rope both head and heels. There was a two-minute time limit and a steer was released every two minutes whether or not the previous contestants had gotten back to the finish line. The biggest difference between those ropings and the one here at Emporia, however, was terrain. This pasture, he said, was almost like an arena compared to the rocks, gullies, and cactus of west Texas.

It seems to me that if you're going to have a pasture roping, that's the way it should be. Contest conditions should be as close as possible to the real thing.

40.   *Curt Brummett, Roping Addict*

MOST people would probably equate failure with ineptitude, but often lack of success indicates instead truly outstanding ability. Baseball fans tell me, for instance, that a pitcher who loses twenty games in a season is often comparable in talent to one who wins twenty games. And how many people do you know who could get fired from the same job three times in one day?

Meet Curt Brummett, a New Mexico cowboy who has worked on ranches and feedlots from Wyoming to Texas. He is also a teller of funny stories, fast gaining a reputation as one of the country's leading cowboy humorists. He's been compared to Will Rogers and Mark Twain, not bad company for a fellow whose English teacher never thought he'd get out of high school. If even half the occurrences he writes about are true (and he has published four or five books and made several tapes), then you wonder how he ever survived his boyhood. The things he's done with tomcats, spooky horses, and homemade hotshots! Not to mention dynamite, windmill towers, pit-bull-blue-heeler-cross dogs, and frijoles.

I met Brummett at the first annual National Cowboy Symposium and Celebration in 1989, a fine event, especially the final session on Sunday afternoon—a team-roping, cutting-horse contest, and team-penning contest. You get everybody from rodeo greats like Jim Shoulders and Tuffy Cooper to cowboy poets like Waddy Mitchell out there on horseback, chasing stock, and having a good old time. I've been back every year, and every year Brummett has mounted me (and anyone else who needs it) in the team roping. And he mounts you well; Old Worthless is the most misnamed horse I've ever had the pleasure of roping off of.

Brummett currently lives back in his home state near Maljamar, which, he points out for those ignorant of geography, is about fifteen miles east of Loco Hills. That's an appropriate location for a man who is crazy to rope. "I've been cussed, yelled at, mistreated, abused, fired,"—he rattles off at least a dozen colorful verbs—"since I was eleven years old because of roping, but I don't want a job if I can't swing a rope."

He swings a good one, both in the jackpot arena and in the pasture. Probably his favorite job ever was near Dalhart, where he was the youngest of four cowboys who were looking after several thousand Louisiana steers that had contracted shipping fever on the trip to the Texas Panhandle. For weeks, they roped and doctored from 150 to 200 head of cattle a day, seven days a week—and then went to jackpot ropings at night.

Each man wore out five horses a day and the four of them went through a coil (six hundred feet) of nylon rope a week. That's some two dozen ropes a week, and I've known some good pasture cowboys who have used the same nylon for years. To keep things interesting they'd put up $25 each, and the first man to miss a loop, either the head or the heels, had to kick in another $25, giving the winner, the last one to miss, $125. During one stretch, they went seven days—something like two thousand throws—before the first miss.

The three-in-a-day firing occurred in a feedlot where Brummett was seen by the owner as he dropped a loop on a recalcitrant heifer. Now it's a known fact that recalcitrance in a bovine can be detected much earlier by a rope-happy cowboy than by a cattle owner, who in this instance told Brummett to collect his pay. But back at the office the foreman told Brummett to get back on his horse, that he was short of good help and would make it all right with the owner.

On his way back down the alley, Brummett saw a notorious fence-crawler, one with a set of inviting horns, and shook out his rope. Just as he bedded him down, figuring to teach the steer a lesson that would make him think twice about getting out again, the owner reappeared. "I thought I fired you," he said. "You did, but the foreman said to get back to work," Brummett replied. "Go get your pay," the owner told him once more.

And once more the foreman told Brummett that he would fix things up, to get back to the pens. Sure enough, once he returned he saw a sick steer, and try as he would Brummett couldn't get the steer to drive. So he shook down his rope and started after him, but just as he did he saw the owner driving up. "I'll put my horse away and go," said Brummett. "No you won't," said the owner. "You'll tie him to the fence right now and throw your saddle in this pickup. I'll drive you to the gate."

A couple of years ago a rancher he had worked for as a teenager was talking to Brummett's wife. "I should have hung that damn kid with his own rope," he said, "but I figured he'd grow out of it." And Sheila's long-suffering response? "He hasn't yet."

Part Seven

BOOTS AND SADDLES

As DO most other occupational folk groups in American culture, cowboys have a distinctive mode of dress, a uniform appropriate to their work. Details of the uniform will vary from region to region and from person to person, but the two most visible—and most universal—components of this livery are a broad-brimmed, high-crowned hat and fancy-topped, high-heeled boots. (I'm speaking somewhat historically here. Today you can see about as many goat-roper caps and flat-heeled "ropers," or even tennis shoes, at a livestock auction, in the pasture, or at a rodeo—at least behind the chutes—as you can western hats and boots. "Why are you wearing tennis shoes instead of boots?" the tourist asked the cowboy back of the bucking chutes. "So I won't be mistaken for a truck driver," he replied.) While both the high-heeled boot and the ten-gallon hat are associated in the popular mind with Texas, neither originated there.

The hat that won the West, for instance, was produced in a Philadelphia factory, the brainchild of a New Jersey man who was walking across Kansas to the goldfields of Colorado when he got the idea. I still remember from my teenage years an old radio "Gunsmoke" episode in which Chester, riding across a hot prairie from Hays City to Dodge, was muttering away, as usual, this time about how nice it would be if somebody would invent a portable shade tree that could be carried along wherever one went. And, if not in his exact words, I can still hear William Conrad's perfect Marshall Dillon voice (I always thought that Hollywood made a big mistake when they didn't give Conrad the television role): "Somebody already has, Chester: John B. Stetson."

The cattle may have come up from Texas and the hats from back east, but Kansas is the home of the cowboy boot. The story goes that a Colorado drover on his way home from the Kansas City Stockyards in 1875 stopped at Charles H. Hyer's cobbler shop in Olathe and ordered a pair of riding boots with some very special features—high scalloped tops, pointed toes, and a tall, slanted heel. This cowboy also, so it's told, had his right boot made from a last fitted to his right foot, his left boot from a last of his left foot. Sounds logical enough, but this was a relatively new technique at the time; many boots worn by cowboys—before (and some after) Hyer— were made from a single last. You got a fit by wading in water, then letting the boots dry around your foot.

How accurate is this traditional account? Well, I figure that if the best a book called *Texas Boots* (by Sharon DeLano and David Rieff) can do is say that Hyer wasn't really the first bootmaker because there was already a shop in Coffeyville making slant-heeled boots as early as the late 1860s (this on the testimony of one of the best of the Texas bootmakers, Henry Leopold, whose father Frederick William Leopold worked in that very Coffeyville shop before moving on to Texas), then Kansas, and the tallgrass country, can safely claim the honor. H. J. Justin's shop, established at Spanish Fort near the Old Chisholm Trail in 1879, appears to have been the first in Texas.

Cowboy boots were an idea whose time had come, and at both ends of the Texas-to-Kansas cattle trails in the late 1870s and early 1880s bootmaking shops sprang up, most of them operated by Germans such as Hyer, Justin, and Leopold. Hyer continued to be a dominant force in the boot industry, making made-to-measure special-order boots as well as standard sizes for the retail trade.

For just over a century Olathe was home not only to the first but also to one of the nation's largest manufacturers of cowboy boots. An old photograph (taken around 1900) of Hyer employees standing in front of the factory shows fifty-five leather-aproned workers. Over the years Hyer made boots for both working cowboys and celebrities—Tom Mix, William S. Hart, Harry Carey, Ruth Roland ("Queen of the Silent Westerns"), Joel McCrea, Clark Gable, and Will Rogers.

One of the order forms for Will Rogers, now in the Johnson County Museum, was made out by a Hyer representative in Beverly Hills who went by to measure Rogers's feet personally.

Charles H. Hyer, maker of the first cowboy boots. (Author's collection.)

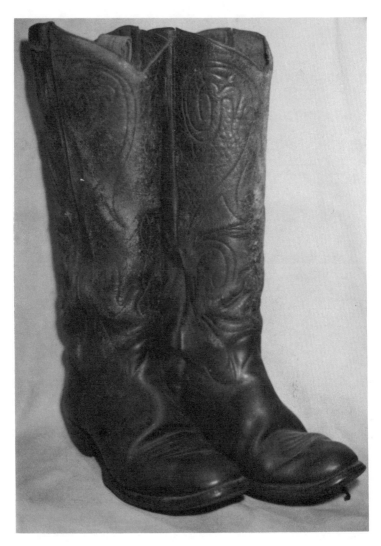

A pair of Hyer boots, c. 1900. (Author's collection.)

(His foot outline, by the way, matches mine.) Rogers ordered two pairs of kangaroo boots with twelve-and-a-half-inch tops, five rows of stitching, flat narrow toes, and one-and-five-eighths-inch medium undershot heels. Here is what the Hyer man wrote on the order form:

> Boys, I sure was glad to get these two orders. He wants them just as light weight as you can make them (he says). He is a funny fellow. [A classic understatement!] Said he did not have any money for a deposit. I told him that we would risk him one more time. He said that he could sell one of his polo horses, the best one, for enough to pay for them. He had on an old pair of boots, just the worst torn up boots I ever saw, just a bunch of holes, and said he had two more pairs at home under the bed that was worn worse than the ones he had on. I went out to his house but he was at a polo field raising hell around like a kid. But he is a good fellow at that.

But even the patronage of celebrities couldn't keep the Hyer Company going forever.

The end came in 1977 when Hyer fell victim to inflation, high labor costs and the rampant urbanization of Johnson County. First the company—lock, stock, lasts, and stitching machines—was bought by the Ben Miller Boot Company, which a few years earlier had started the Larry Mahan Boot Collection, a diversifying move on the part of the eight-time world champion rodeo cowboy and one-man conglomerate. A year later everything was moved to El Paso, close to cheap labor. Hyer was swallowed up whole and, as far as I have been able to find out, you can't buy a Hyer boot anymore.

Not that I had ever bought a Hyer boot in the first place. I have always liked Bluchers, also made (until 1970) in Olathe. The first pair of boots I remember owning (at around age five or six) were brown and short-topped with a red steer head in front and back. They were probably bought one Saturday night in Cottonwood Falls from Jim Bell and Son, but I don't remember what company made them.

My father's first pair of boots were more memorable. He and my uncle were reared on a small Flint Hills stock ranch near Cassoday and they took to working with horses, mules, cows, and calves at an early age. When Dad was around ten or twelve (Uncle Marshall was three years behind him), a neighbor sent over a horse for them to break (the first of hundreds they would tame over the next three-quarters of a century). Dad doesn't remember just how much they got for breaking that horse—five or ten dollars—but it was enough to send off for a pair of catalog boots. One pair. Deciding who wore them, however, was no real problem. Whenever they got a horse to break, whoever rode first to take the buck out of him got to wear the boots.

Uncle Marshall's feet are of a reasonably normal shape, so he can buy boots off the shelf, although, like many cowboys, he prefers them custom-made. Dad and I, though, both have a high instep, which leads to a real problem. Not just one of fit, but also of looks.

Traditionally, Old West cowboys were as vain of their small feet and high-arched, smooth-fitting boots (associated with riding a horse, as opposed to the big feet and flat, clumpy boots of farmers following a plow) as any woman, a character flaw (or strength) with which I am afflicted. I hate to buy boots off the shelf because, in order to get them over my instep, I have to buy them a couple of sizes too big. Or else, like a pair of Tony Lama ropers I bought from Jim's Cowboy Shop here in Emporia, I have to order a seven-and-a-half double E, then for two weeks or more have Jim stretch the width up into the instep. It's much easier and more comfortable, if more expensive, to have boots made to order. But what the heck, as an old friend (Stanley Stout—no need to let him get away with anonymity) likes to say, "Go first class. It only costs eighty percent more."

I started this chapter talking about boots and hats, so I'll end it the same way. Cowboys, it seems to me, both from my study of the Old West and from my observation of the contemporary scene, tend essentially to be either hat men or boot men. If you want to tell one from the other, catch them when they're in bed (asleep or otherwise occupied) and yell "Fire!" (or some other suitable alarm). Me? I'll grab my boots first.

42.   *Cowboy Pants*

(1987)

I REMEMBER a bumper sticker that coincided with the peak of the urban cowboy craze a few years back—"I'm not a cowboy, I just found the hat"—probably a hat thrown away in disgust by a real cowboy at the thought of all the gunsels playing songs by Alabama on the jukebox in some obscure Kansas 3.2 beer joint. The hat is the most recognizable part of the cowboy uniform, with boots coming in a close second, both items easily acquired by the would-be who wouldn't know a nylon from a silk manila if he were using one to try to rope a mechanical bull.

It has to be as galling to feedlot cowboys as to working ranch hands from the Gypsum, Smoky, or Flint hills to see an eighty-five-dollar Resistol and some two-hundred-dollar Tony Lamas on a Wichita yuppie who doesn't even know what kind of pants to wear. Real cowboys might suffer through some Lee Greenwood or Oak Ridge Boys in order to do a little belt buckle polishing at the rodeo dance, but designer jeans? Spare me.

No, if you want to come across as the genuine article, you have to have some sweat stains on your hat, some manure on your boots, and the right design on your rear pockets. Now I've known a few working cowboys to wear off-brand jeans or even bib overalls, while a lot of ranchers and cattlemen (who may or may not be cowboys) will wear khakis, but most cowboys wear one of three brands of pants (older cowboys, especially, don't like the term jeans)—Levi's, Lee Riders, or Wranglers.

Older cowboys tend to wear Levi's, the original blue denim cowboy pants (from *serge de Nîmes,* a heavy cotton cloth manufactured in France) and most probably the ones they grew up with. Sometime in the later nineteenth or early twentieth century, well after erstwhile prospector Levi Strauss first turned his tenting material into pants for California gold miners in 1853, cowboys discovered that Levi's unshrunk, blue-dyed pants were good in the saddle. They wore well and didn't ride up the leg the way softer material did. The rest of the country discovered Levi's in the 1930s when dude ranch guests took them back east and when cowboy movie stars (including Reb Russell and John Wayne) adopted them as standard gear. Thus was begun the movement that put Levi's not only on cowboys but on people from every other facet of American society—and won them a permanent exhibit in the Americana wing of the Smithsonian.

Partially because of this wide adoption by those outside the guild, although probably more because of peer pressure and intense advertising, many of today's younger cowboys, especially rodeo cowboys, have never worn a pair of Levi's. Instead their uniform is Wranglers, manufactured by Blue Bell, Inc., of Greensboro, North Carolina, one of professional rodeo's largest corporate sponsors. Blue Bell started out in 1904 making bib overalls for southern farmers; the company grew steadily and expanded into other lines of clothing over the years. As did the others of the Big Three, Blue Bell produced millions of military uniforms during World War II.

In 1947 under J. C. Fox, who was president of the company from 1937 to 1948 and who had gotten his start in the family overall business in Atchison, Kansas, Blue Bell began to manufacture western pants. A year later Blue Bell made a cagey move to win acceptance in the rodeo fraternity, an even more tightknit and clannish bunch in the late forties than today. The company paid top contestants (usually world champions such as Jim Shoulders or Gerald Roberts) to wear and promote Wranglers. At the same time they went for the youth market by including small comic books (some with covers drawn by Peter Hurd) with each pair of new pants. I thought the stories, detailing adventures of rodeo or range, were more than a little hokey and usually threw the books away with the labels as I ripped them off a new pair, but I do remember keeping one about Ross Dollarhide around for a while, probably because of the name, which I thought at the time surely had to be made up. Those little books, like old baseball cards, are undoubtedly collector's items today; a complete set is probably worth more than old Ross's total winnings back in the days of five dollar entry fees.

Although I wear all three brands more or less interchangeably, my favorite pants are Lee Riders, which, like the cowboy boot, originated in Kansas. Vermonter Henry David Lee (1849–1928) moved west for his health, establishing a mercantile company in Salina in 1889. Besides becoming one of the leading wholesale grocers in the region, Lee also sold school supplies, hardware, notions, and dry goods—including overalls. By 1911 Lee was manufacturing overalls, jackets, and dungarees in Salina and two years later he had invented the Union-All, a one-piece denim work suit that could readily be slipped on over other clothing.

In 1924 the Lee company introduced its first pair of pants for the cowboy market and two years later the first zippered fly model (a mistake, in my opinion), although they continued to sell button models as well. In fact, I can remember when you could buy both Lees and Wranglers with buttons. (I can also remember going into Haberlein's Men's Store in El Dorado to buy my first pair of Levi's—for just under three dollars.)

Maybe one reason Lees fit so well was because the company got some design advice from a woman with a real knack for form-fitting costumes—fan dancer Sally Rand. Rand was married to rodeo cowboy Turk Greenough, who, while competing at a Kansas City rodeo in the early 1940s, was invited out to the local plant to give some suggestions on improving the fit. Rand got involved with the project, ripping up pairs of pants and pinning them back up on her husband until she came up with a snug design she liked.

In 1946, about the time that Wrangler was getting into the market, Lee placed the industry's first national advertising (in *Life*) for western wear, just as it had been first (in 1917) to advertise work clothing nationally. As Wrangler began to make serious inroads into rodeo sales in the 1950s, Lee responded with some big-name endorsements of its own—from hands like Guy Weeks and Casey Tibbs. Kansan Bobby Berger was the rodeo spokesman for Lee during the 1970s, billed as the "Lee Rider" and featured in much of the company's national advertising.

The company was no newcomer to this approach, however, having used the entire "Our Gang" cast, including the dog, in advertisements for Lee Whizit Playsuits in 1928. That same year Babe Ruth appeared in an ad for a set of Lee Whizit Union-Alls. He was shown working on a car with the Union-Alls slipped over his shirt and tie and is quoted as saying, "There's as much speed to a Lee Whizit as there is on Walter Johnson's fast ball. Both are on you before you know it."

In 1969 Lee, which maintains its headquarters in Johnson County (and has had an office of some sort or other in the Kansas City area since 1915), was acquired by the VF Corporation of Pennsylvania, which claims to be the world's largest publicly held apparel company; Lee claims to be the world's second-largest producer of jeans. Blue Bell says that it is the nation's second largest apparel manufacturer, although whether second to VF or to privately held Levi Strauss is not clear. Levi Strauss without question makes more cowboy pants than either of its two chief competitors.

Volume, however, is really a moot question as far as I'm concerned—all three are good cowboy brands. So let's round up all the jeans made by Calvin and Gloria—and all the pseudocountry records while we're at it—and ship the whole caboodle down to Gilley's for use by the urban cowboys.

Postscript

Since the above was first written, the Lee Company has been taken over by Blue Bell. Apparently, or so it seems to me, because Blue Bell already has the rodeo market sewed up, Lee Riders have been turned into yuppie jeans. At least I haven't been able to find a good pair of eleven-ounce denim, straight-legged Lee Riders in either Bluestem Farm and Ranch Supply or Jim Bell's Men and Boys Wear for about three years. And I just don't go for the polyester stretch or the stone-washed versions, so I've gone back to wearing

Levi's. Maybe I ought to go out and buy a shelf full of shrink-
to-fit 501s before they take them off the market—and hope
that my waist size doesn't undergo any major changes.

43. *Hatman Jack*

EVERY cowboy knows that, except for pants, if you want the
best you generally get it custom made. You might have only
enough money to outfit yourself with some Justins off the
shelf or a pretty good used Longhorn saddle, but there is
always the someday-hope for a pair of Bluchers with your own
brand inlaid into the tops by an artisan who has sewn them by
hand for your feet alone, or for a Moss or a Donaho saddle
shaped to fit your horse and your body.

Hats, on the other hand—well, everybody knows that hats
are made in big factories and if you want to get one to look
right you're just going to have to steam it and reshape it and
wear it in the rain a time or two.

At least that's what I used to think until I met Hatman
Jack back in 1987. A native of Caldwell, where Texas longhorns met Kansas trains over a century ago, Jack Kellogg, not
yet thirty years old, has been operating the Wichita Hat
Works since 1981. He can whip up a piece of felt or panama
into a fedora, a derby, or a Tom Mix special—any shape you
want, as fancy as you please. And surprisingly reasonable,
compared to the price differential between shop-made and
shelf boots.

I've interviewed several bootmakers in recent years and
am fairly familiar with lasts and crimp boards and finishers,
but Hatman Jack's shop provided my first up-close view of
flanges and blocks and stretchers and brim cutters. I also
picked up a new technical term: "pounce." Pouncing a hat is
not jumping on it like a cat, but sandpapering the felt to the
proper finish.

As with a boot, a custom-made hat starts with a measurement, but whereas bootmakers often have to write down just the design the customer wants, Jack told me that many of his patrons depend on him to advise them on color and size and shape and design. Despite the relatively modest size of his operation, his clientele includes such diverse singing stars as bluesman B. B. King, western swing pioneer Leon McAuliffe, and current country music star Gene Watson. He wouldn't come right out and say so, but I think his favorite customers are Ranger Doug and Too Slim of the neo-sagebrush Riders in the Sky trio, partly because these sons of the Sons of the Pioneers go in for the traditional high-crowned Montana-style hats but mainly because Jack himself plays accordion (and sometimes yodels) for the Rhythm Rangers, a band that plays old-time western and country honky-tonk music.

Hatman himself is solidly grounded in tradition. He hand stitches leather hatbands rather than using a machine, for instance, because it's the old-fashioned way of doing it—and it gives him more control over quality. He also talks of how you used to be able to locate a man by his hat style—the curled brim of the Southwest, the high crown of the North Country, the flat low crown of the southern gambler—differences that have blurred in recent years as television and movies have homogenized the West.

Although the customer is usually right, Jack has had occasion to resist some innovations, such as one man's request that he sew zipper bags inside his leather hatband; Jack just couldn't think of anything legal that could be put in them. Then there was the silversmith who wanted small holes built into the brim so he could keep his tools in his hat as he worked. Jack refused; he couldn't stand the thought of one of his hats perforated before it even left the shop.

When I saw Hatman Jack in the spring of 1988, he was on his way to Bloomingdale's, that shopping mecca for New York yuppies, where he hoped to pick up some orders, then go back twice a year to deliver hats and take more orders. I haven't had a chance to talk to him since, but I have a feeling that there will be a lot of 5X beaver fur flying around the Wichita Hat Works this fall.

44. *Tony Lama Boots*

ALTHOUGH I generally prefer to get my boots custom made, I have on occasion bought a pair off the shelf, particularly ropers. My favorite pair of those were Tony Lamas, some of the best factory-made boots available. During the past few years I have visited a number of custom bootmakers, so in April of 1987 when I was in El Paso I took the opportunity to see the other side of the business, to visit the world's largest mass-producer of handcrafted boots.

Often, especially in a crafted product such as cowboy boots, volume means mediocrity, but I was honestly surprised at the amount of handwork that goes into Tony Lamas, especially considering that the factory turns out an average of something like 2,200 pairs a day—and has at times done nearly twice that. I was also impressed with the quality of material that goes into a Tony Lama boot. Except for the nylon pulls and thread, the steel shank, and a piece of plastic designed to connect the heel to the uppers, everything is natural—real leather and real wooden pegs in the soles.

Having called ahead to arrange a tour of the plant, I arrived at 7:30 A.M. and walked down a hallway lined with photographs of famous Lama customers—Western movie stars, country music singers, and rodeo performers—to the office of Dan Ponder, a twenty-six-year-old boot designer who had joined the firm eight years earlier as a salesman. Ponder gave me a short history of the company (founded in 1911), then hung a badge from my shirt pocket (just like on the television cop shows) and took me on a tour of the 194,000 square foot facility. Offices and fitting rooms are on the east end of the lasting and top-work building, while bottoms and finishing are done in an adjoining building, a drying room connecting the two. Shipping facilities are housed separately.

Already the plant was in full operation, some nine hundred employees cutting, stitching, gluing, and nailing. The movement was fast but deliberate, the atmosphere purposeful not frantic. Computerized stitching machines were sewing flawless designs on boot tops, and other operations I had seen performed by hand at custom shops were done by machine here (machines, I was told, Tony Lama himself had designed). Handwork was done smoothly but rapidly; I can still see in my mind's eye one man tossing a handful of tacks into his mouth, then taking one after another out with his left hand and hammering each once with his right hand nearly as fast as the eye could follow.

Efficiency is practiced not only in labor but in materials. Just as a packing plant uses everything from the hog but the squeal, so Lama uses nearly every bit of leather that comes in the front door—on belts, purses, and key rings if not on boots. Dealers for their products are found in every state, as well as in such exotic locales as Japan, Australia, France, and Arabia.

There may be nine hundred employees at Tony Lama, compared to from one to a dozen in a custom shop, and they may use computerized stitchers and automated assembly lines, but the basic process in bootmaking is the same for either type of operation. Quality of material and skill in construction are the key differences between a good shelf boot and one that falls apart the first time you walk through a wet barn lot.

45. *The Donaho Saddlery*

AT THE 1990 National Cowboy Symposium and Celebration I paused for a moment at the display of the R. E. Donaho Saddlery, which is celebrating its centennial anniversary this year. I had not run across the Donaho saddle before, but then the West is filled with custom saddlemakers, good ones, who never attain the widespread reputation, or the sales, of a Hamley or a Bona Allen or an S. D. Myers. As I talked to Rector Story, current owner, I learned a lot about saddlemaking in general and Donaho saddles in particular.

For one thing, the Donaho Saddlery is actually older than

a century (no one knows for sure just when it did start) and it has operated under half a dozen names, but it has always been located in the original city block of San Angelo, Texas, and since 1890 it has always been owned by someone who learned the trade in the shop. Donaho, for instance, started working in the R. J. Andrews Saddlery in 1907 and bought it in 1936 when Andrews died. Two years later Story, nineteen at the time, went to work there and then bought the shop in 1954 when Donaho died. Unlike all the other owners, however, Story didn't change the name when he acquired the business.

Back in 1936 the shop was still making a few old fashioned saddles—large square pointed skirts, stirrup leathers on the outside of the fender, border stamped. Today Story is making fifty special centennial saddles with this old-time look. In the intervening years he has seen many styles come and go—the low Mexican "pelican" horn, the two-rope horn, the high-post dally horn; the Cheyenne roll; the slick fork, low cantle roping saddle; the return to a higher cantle and more swell. In fact, Story believes, saddlers today are making the most practical saddle in years—the cantle neither too low nor too high; the swells neither too wide nor too narrow.

Older cowboys sometimes complain that today's saddle trees aren't as good as they used to be, but, Story says, they are actually better: "Someone tells me, 'I never broke a tree before,' and I tell him, 'You didn't have a nylon rope before, either.'" Another change is in size of people. When he first went to work for the company, most people ordered thirteen- or fourteen-inch seats; today sixteen inches is the most common.

The half dozen employees of Donaho make about 250 saddles a year, down from a peak of four hundred back when both the oil and cattle markets were booming. Most of these saddles are sold in Texas, but the company sells from coast to coast, with New Mexico and the Dakotas being good markets. "The drought of the 1950s did more than anything to spread us around," Story told me. "A lot of Texas cattlemen bought ranches in the Dakotas or Montana and they took our saddles up with them. When they'd come back for cattle or horses, some of the northern hands would come along, and we'd always get a bunch of orders from them."

I asked about his most unusual order, and Story laughed and told me about a navy commander who had retired to the family ranch with his wife, an ex-Broadway showgirl. But she couldn't ride horses because of a back injury: the bone at the base of her spine turned at a right angle and jutted out nearly an inch. One day the old commander walked into the Donaho shop with his wife and barked an order to Story—"Now feel this!"—and shoved the young saddlemaker's hand right down on his wife's bottom so he could feel the protruding bone. Story made a special saddle with a slot up the back of the cantle, even though Donaho, who was still in charge, thought the saddle would break. Today, however, that saddle is still in use on the ranch, long after the death of the woman for whom it was built.

"I never had a man working for me that I didn't learn something from," Story told me. "Anytime a man thinks he knows all there is to know about saddles, that's when he starts going downhill." It seems to me that that's a pretty good philosophy for life in general.

46.   *Russell Moss, Horseman and Saddler*

BACK IN 1985 I found myself in Kansas City with a little free time, so I went over to the stockyards to watch them sell cattle. The auction hadn't started yet, so I wandered down Genessee Street, looking for signs of the old Shipley store, at one time one of the world's largest stockmen's supply companies. Shipley is gone, but I did happen upon a saddle shop, so I walked in. Saddle trees and saddles to be repaired and a new saddle shared with a display counter and cash register the front part of the narrow room. Toward the back, a man with a leather-working apron was on the phone, and while he talked a large Doberman trotted out past him, looked me over thoroughly, then trotted back out of sight. After a few minutes the man hung up the phone and asked if he could help me. I asked a few questions—about how long he had been making saddles, how he got started—and I soon knew he had a story to tell, so I began making some notes.

Russell Moss was born at Montmar, Missouri, in 1911, son of a foreman on a big farm. There were always lots of horses on the place, and Moss recalls the time a man showed up for a job with an old Stetson, chaps, spurs, a pistol—the works. "If you can't live up to that stuff, just put it back in the box and keep traveling," Moss recalls his father saying. In reply the new hand roped an unbroken roan horse out of the herd in the corral, threw a trip on him, put a jacket over his eyes, saddled him, and stepped on him and spurred until he quit bucking. Next he pulled his gun out and fired it until the horse quit jumping at the noise, then rode him some half a dozen miles into town and back. On his return, Moss said, the roan was walking calmly, already broke to rein.

Moss also recalled the Sunday afternoon impromptu bronc ridings on their place, especially the man who insisted that his bucking horse be anchored with a hundred-foot piece of haymow rope. When the horse came to the end of the rope, the would-be rider went another hundred feet into the air, or so it seemed to the spectators. Then there was the hired man, afflicted with a stutter, who failed to get the corral gate shut on an angered bovine. As the steer chased him toward the house, Mrs. Moss, who was shelling peas on the porch, ran inside and slammed the door as the hired man circled the house shouting, "B-b-by G-god, Jennie, o-open the d-d-door and l-l-let m-me in!"

With that kind of background it is no wonder that young Russell got into the rodeo and Wild West show business, riding with Roy Knapp and his Roughriders during the later 1920s and 1930s. He did some trick riding, including a three-horse Roman-riding act, and also trained show horses for other trick riders. His method of training was to get the horse to respond (as does a dog) because it wants to please, not because of fear. And, he said, avoid a narrow-eyed horse (not enough room for brains) with a lot of white in the eyes (too flighty and nervous).

At one time he worked with trick rider Pinky Branoski (stage name Barnes) who did a lot of stunt double work in movies. Sometimes Barnes would get double-booked, so Moss, who knew Barnes's routines, would wear a similar costume and put on the show. No one ever called them on the substitution. Barnes, Moss told me, was an excellent horseman, but Knapp wasn't so good, although he liked to dress the part. Perhaps as a result of his father's attitude about living up to one's appearance, Moss once lent a good palomino he owned to Knapp to ride in a parade—but he didn't tell him how the horse would react to spurs, especially ones with big fancy rowels. After the first block, Knapp led the horse for the rest of the parade.

Moss also worked for the Panhandle Slim Wild West Show around 1930. Slim (real name Buford Raider), who had ridden for the 101 show, had bought out Tim McCoy's outfit and was traveling the country with a couple of bucking bulls and broncs and some roping and dogging cattle and a Roman-riding team. It cost a quarter to get in to watch Moss do trick riding and a black cowboy known as Chocolate Drop ride broncs and bulls. Moss didn't know his real name, only that he was an excellent rider and had spent some time in the Texas penitentiary.

Moss got his start in saddlemaking by working (free) on weekends at the shop of renowned saddler Monroe Veach in Trenton, Missouri. When he asked for a full-time job, Veach told Moss that he couldn't afford to hire him because he had learned too much, that he should be in business for himself. So Veach gave him a saddle tree and a bunch of leather and Moss bought a used sewing machine and set up shop in Kansas City. After making a saddle with these materials, Moss opened up for business on a Sunday afternoon. This was just after the war when people were eager to get some new equipment. He sold not only his new saddle that day, but took orders for four more.

Later in 1945 he moved to Chanute, the nicest town he ever lived in, he said, and worked there until the early 1950s, when he moved the shop to Coffeyville. In 1961 he moved back to Kansas City, where he has been making and selling saddles ever since.

47. *Ken Spain, Saddle Man*

NOT LONG AGO I got a real education in the history of saddles. Oh, I've watched fashions change in my lifetime, from the slick-forked, low-cantled roping saddles favored in the early 1950s to today's saddles, many of which are actually built on association bronc trees. And I had some idea of earlier styles from the high-backed, wide-swelled Mueller bronc-riding saddles my father and uncle bought in the 1930s and from the old Frazier nickel-horned saddle my grandfather rode. But I had no clear conception of the evolution of the western stock saddle until I visited with Ken Spain down in Aledo, Texas, in the first part of October 1990.

I had actually gone down to see a pair of Coffeyville boots in Spain's possession, but his real passion is collecting old saddles. Very old saddles. He has about thirty of them, most made in the nineteenth century. And, in his unpretentious, quiet way, he is a walking encyclopedia of saddle lore. I learned that while the Great Plains stock saddle may have had its ultimate origin in the equipment of Mexican vaqueros, its real history begins in Kansas Territory in the Denver shop of E. L. Gallatin. This was in 1860, and a couple of years later he took in a partner, Francis Gallup, who later paired up for a time with Frazier. By 1867 Gallatin had moved his shop to Cheyenne, where a number of influential saddlers operated before the turn of the century. The Cheyenne saddle evolved into today's western stock saddle.

Chief among the Cheyenne saddlers was F. A. Meanea, Gallatin's nephew, who bought him out in 1881. A "Meanie" saddle was, Spain says, the major status symbol among plains cowboys. The Meanea shop closed in 1928. Spain owns several Meanie saddles, and also several made by the Collins Brothers, who moved from Omaha to Fort Laramie to Cheyenne, where they were in business by 1876. He does not—yet—own a Gallatin saddle, although he has his eye on one.

When I arrived at the offices of Spain's wire and cable company, we visited a while in his office, then drove down to a bank in the old stockyards area of north Fort Worth to see the boots and about a dozen saddles he had on display there. Among them was an 1885 Collins saddle with built-in saddle bags made of buffalo hide, the long, shaggy hair still attached. There was also a Meanea saddle of the style that Charles M. Russell always rode. Three other Meanies were on display, including a "citizen" saddle, built light for riding but not guaranteed for roping.

The most interesting saddle, however, was a Mexican saddle built around 1850, before blanket or sheepskin linings had been introduced. This innovation, Spain said, came with the post–Civil War trail drives, when nighttime stampedes meant that cowboys had no time to get a blanket under the saddle in the dark, but a bare saddle could ruin a horse's back in minutes. Until he bought it a couple of years ago, this saddle had never been more than fifty miles from Mora, New Mexico, and it was still being used, almost daily, by two children on their kid horse, nearly a century and a half after it had been made.

"Where are all the Texas saddles?" his fellow citizens often ask when Spain displays his collection. "Why were all the saddle shops up north?" I had wondered about this myself, and Spain's response made sense: the saddlemakers built their shops at the end of the trail, where the cowboys got paid, figuring that a few of them, at least, would buy a new rig with their hard-earned pay instead of blowing it all on wine, women, and song.

And the Coffeyville boots? I saw them, too, but by that time I was more interested in saddles. Ken Spain's enthusiasm is catching.

48. *J. W. Cubine and the Coffeyville Boot*

IN THE century and a quarter that has passed since the cow-
boy was born in the Texas-to-Kansas trail drives that followed
the Civil War, the West has known many famous bootmakers:
Charles H. Hyer; H. J. Justin; Gus Blucher and Archer
LaForce, who left the employ of Justin in 1915 to open a shop
in Cheyenne. Three years later Blucher would move to
Olathe, right across the street from Hyer, while LaForce eventually settled in Tucson, where he founded the Western Boot
Company. Leopold, Leddy, Olsen-Steltzer, Tony Lama, Paul
Bond—the list goes on and on. But in all the West only the
Coffeyville boot was so popular, its fame so widespread, its
qualities so well known, that it became, like Levi Strauss's
famous pants, nearly generic, even finding its way into a
cowboy folk song, "The Dad-Blamed Boss": "I'll get me a new
slicker and some Coffeyville Boots / Buy a quart of good red
licker and quit this crazy old galoot."

Coffeyville. Now there's a name to reckon with in western
history. Home of the Daltons and site of their ill-fated attempt to rob two banks simultaneously back on October 5,
1892. Home, also, of rancher and movie star Reb Russell (see
chapter 4). Most important, Coffeyville was one of the early
Kansas cow towns that helped to develop the image, and the
reality, of the cowboy.

From 1871 to 1873 scores of thousands of cattle were
shipped to market from Coffeyville on the Leavenworth,
Lawrence, and Galveston Railroad and, although the flow
tapered off after that, Coffeyville continued for years to be a
town that catered to the cattle trade. Newspaper ads from the
1870s hawked merchants' wares: pants and hats, saddles and
harness, groceries and supplies. "General outfitting for the
Texas trade and the Cherokee Nation," proclaimed Bar-
ricklow and Brothers Dry Goods Store. Closer to the stockyards, Red Hot Street lived up to its name as the drovers
quenched their thirst at establishments such as the Legal
Tender Billiard Hall ("good beer at lowest prices") or the
Keg Saloon, or at Schmitt's Brewery in nearby Parker. Even

the Star Bakery favored the cowboys, selling whiskey, wine, beer, and cigars along with its pies and cakes.

No one knows just when the first bootmaker came to Coffeyville, but boots and saddles were items cowboys often needed at the end of a drive, so it was natural for merchants and artisans to set up shop at the point where the trailhand collected his wages. Up until the development of the western boot in the mid-1870s, the drovers wore a military-style boot: stovepipe top, flat round toe, flat low heel. The Coffeyville boot was a transitional boot (as were the earliest boots made by Hyer and Justin), an adaptation of the cavalry boot for the needs of the drover. The top was high and plain but, instead of a scallop in front and back, the Coffeyville boot was straight across the back and had a one-piece front that rounded up into an arch reaching toward the knee. Often a red star was sewn onto this half-circle of leather at the top, a decoration sure to attract the eye of a Lone Star rider. The toe was round, but more pointed and less flat than that of a military boot, and the heel was built up and slanted in. Right and left boots were made on different lasts—an innovation attributed to both the Coffeyville boot and Charles Hyer.

By some accounts the Coffeyville boot was first introduced in the late 1860s, but that is most unlikely because Coffeyville itself did not come into existence until 1870, with the cattle trade there reaching its peak in the first half of that decade. More likely this new style emerged in the mid-1870s, when at least two custom boot- and shoemakers had set up shop there. The earlier of these was William Bright, who commenced work sometime between the founding of the town and October 30, 1875, when the first advertisement for his services appeared in the *Coffeyville Journal*.

Did Bright originate the distinctive Coffeyville boot? Or was it, more likely, the brainchild of John W. Cubine, who opened his doors a year later on October 7, 1876? There is no way of knowing for sure, but Cubine was clearly the more successful and innovative craftsman. By 1879, for instance, he had moved to larger quarters and was using tanned alligator hide, "the first we ever saw," according to the newspaper editor. In 1882, Bright was still running the same small ad he had used seven years earlier—"Does good, neat, substantial work"—while Cubine's establishment was booming, proclaiming itself in a large ad as "The Old Reliable Boot and Shoe Shop" and promising top work in the best styles with "Guaranteed Fit and Satisfaction."

According to Wesley Stout, Cubine was indeed the master bootmaker of Coffeyville. Stout, in an article entitled "The Boot that Made Coffeyville Famous," which appeared in the *Coffeyville Journal* on September 29, 1913, recounts a visit to a cow camp in interior Utah, "150 miles from a railroad," where he noted some of the cowboys wearing boots of an identical pattern. In response to his question about where they got such good boots, one of the punchers replied, "They are made to order for us at Coffeyville, Kansas. All the boys around here wear Cubine boots." By this time styles had changed, and Cubine was making scallop-topped cowboy boots instead of the earlier classic one-piece-front, round-topped Coffeyville boot.

J. W. Cubine died in 1911, at which point his son Claude gave up his acting career and took over the business. In the years between 1876 and its eventual closing in 1931, the Cubine shop sold boots in every state west of the Mississippi and in Canada, Alaska, Mexico, and South Africa, as well. One pair of fancy riding boots was even sent to a customer in Paris. Cubine seems not to have attracted celebrity customers in the way that the Hyer and Justin establishments did, although some of the Daltons did buy Cubine boots. This was before they attempted the 1892 raid that made them famous and left two of the three outlaw brothers dead. George Cubine, a worker in his uncle's shop, was one of four Coffeyville defenders killed in the gun battle that day.

Although J. W. Cubine's boots were worn throughout the West, his bread-and-butter customers were the cowboys of the Osage Hills that lay to the southwest of Coffeyville. Cubine sold some 372 pairs of boots in 1891, according to a surviving order book now in the possession of his great-granddaughter, Jackie Barrett of Neodesha, Kansas. This was about the time that Stanley Barnes became head bootmaker for the firm, which was then turning out an average of 7 pairs of fully handmade boots each week, a figure that would quadruple within two decades. Orders were recorded in 1891 for cowboys as far away as Arizona, but the vast majority were from Indian Territory. Among his customers were members of the Cherokee, Delaware, Osage, and Kaw tribes, with several entries referring to the "Delaware payment" or the "Osage payment." The distribution of government annuities was apparently a major time for boot sales.

Scanning through this old order book provides insight into how the reputation of the Coffeyville boot was spread. John Meritt of Winslow, Arizona Territory, for instance, wrote: "I want a genuine cowboy's boot like the ones you have been making for some punchers at Flagstaff." Among these punchers was A. J. Diamond, who ordered three pairs of Cubine boots in 1891. On his first order he wrote: "Send a pair of boots as soon as you can. I like the others very much excepting that they hurt my bunions. If you remember, my boots were made by Ed Geddes measure." Diamond had apparently tried on the boots that Cubine had made for Geddes and ordered a pair just like them, but the new boots fit a bit tighter than the ones that had already been broken in. On this order he instructs Cubine to make the boots a bit larger in the leg and the instep. After his new boots arrived, Diamond gave away the original, tighter pair and in the process Cubine acquired a new customer, for on his second order for 1891 Diamond wrote: "Your boots are just the thing. I let one of my boys have the old ones and he wanted me to order him a pair. He wants them made just as you made the first pair for me only a fraction shorter and some higher in the instep." He then goes on to vouch for his cowhand's credit: "He is alright. Send in my care and make at once."

The most interesting order came from a man named Henry Clark, who did his best to finagle the cost downward: "Make as soon as you can and as cheap as can. These are my wedding boots. The other boots I took more for an accommodation than anything else. Bear that in mind when you price the others." If Clark's miserly impulses toward his boot-maker are indicative of his overall character, then his new wife was in for a tough haul. After all, a new pair of Cubine dress boots made to order from the finest leather cost only nine dollars.

The fame of the Coffeyville boot lingered long after the death of J. W. Cubine. In 1924, for instance, an official of the Henry Bragg Leather Company of St. Joseph, Missouri, wrote to Claude Cubine, commending the work of his father: "We remember quite distinctly the time he was making boots. This is a record that you should be proud of." Two years later a Texas rancher requested an order blank for a pair of Cu-bine boots after a hiatus of twenty-one years: "Your house made my boots for fifteen years up to 1905. Since that time I have tried several makes, but none like the old reliable J. W. Cubine cowboy boot. Hoping that you are still in business, I remain as ever, Yours, J. M. Pharis, Sonora, Texas."

The Old Reliable Boot and Shoe Company has been out of business for well over half a century now, and today few peo-ple, even in Coffeyville, know the name of J. W. Cubine, but the boot he pioneered has achieved world-wide recognition. On a trip to Australia in 1990 I went into a farm-supply store in outback Queensland and there, in an outfitter's brochure, was a drawing and a short account of the Coffeyville boot.

Today you can buy a reproduction Coffeyville boot, com-plete with a red star on the top, through dealers that special-ize in authentic recreations, but if you want a pair of the real McCoy the supply is decidedly limited. In fact, I have been able to learn of the existence of only one pair of the old round-topped Coffeyville boots; they are owned by Ken Spain (see chapter 47). These boots are in remarkably good condi-tion, considering that they are well over a hundred years old. At the time he bought them, Spain thought they were Civil War boots. He has since discovered that his fortuitous pur-chase may well be one of the last surviving links to the trail-driving days of the Old West—and perhaps the earliest surviv-ing example of the cowboy boot.

Subject Index